HONOURING THE FEW

HONOURING THE FEW

The remarkable story of the Battle of Britain heroes and our tribute to them

General Editor: RUPERT PRIOR

FOREWORD BY RT HON LORD TEBBIT CH

BATTLE OF BRITAIN BOOKS

First published in the United Kingdom in 2005 by
Battle of Britain Books, 16 De Beauvoir Square,
London N1 4LD

British Library Cataloguing in Publication Data
A catalogue record for this book is available from the
British Library

ISBN 0-9551351-0-9

Designer: Anne Wilson

Printed and bound by Butler and Tanner, Somerset

PAGE 1 *Touched by history*: the fast interceptor fighter was the backbone of RAF Fighter Command.

PAGE 2 *Monument*: detail of Paul Day's sculpture on London's Embankment.

PAGE 3 *War pilots*: aircrew scramble for the press during a pre-war exercise.

ABOVE *Vapour trails*: the Luftwaffe sent over a mixed force of fighters and bombers in daylight and night raids during the battle.

RIGHT *R4118*: a Mk I Hurricane flown in 49 sorties and involved in the loss of five enemy aircraft in the battle. Now superbly restored by Peter Vacher.

CONTENTS

FOREWORD

by Rt Hon Lord Tebbit CH

It was Bill Bond, the founder of The Battle of Britain Historical Society, who conceived the idea of a Monument to those who won what we now know was the turning point battle of the Second World War. Had it been lost, Britain would have been invaded and all Europe would have been under Nazi, Fascist or Communist rule.

The purpose of the Monument is to ensure that so long as London remains a city, this historic battle, and those who fought and won will not be forgotten. Sited on Victoria Embankment by Westminster Pier it is at the heart of the city which suffered so much by bombing and saw so much of the Battle.

Once the site had been identified, with the help of English Heritage, and generously made available by Westminster City Council, architects were appointed, fund raising began and a design competition organised. The contest was won by Paul Day, a young English sculptor working in France.

Amongst Paul Day's sources for inspiration was the Bayeux Tapestry telling the story of the Battle of Hastings. His magnificent bronze panels tell the story of the Battle of Britain, fought at times over Hastings itself, depicting not only scenes of air combat but events on the ground below. A group of pilots leap out of the bronzes; larger than life.

The panels show anti-aircraft gunners, Spitfires being built and serviced for flight, civilians in the shelters and casualties being dug from the rubble of bombed buildings.

The badges of the squadrons and the names of all the men who flew in action appear, together with those of R.J. Mitchell and Sydney Camm, designers of the Spitfires and Hurricanes which carried the brunt of the fighting.

There can be no doubt of the historical significance of the Battle. It did not decide the outcome of the Second World War but it halted the previously unstoppable Nazi war machine in its tracks giving the Allied Democratic Nations time to gather strength to defeat Nazi Germany.

Thus was the future of the continent of Europe saved from what Churchill called '...the abyss of a new Dark Age made more sinister by the lights of perverted science'. The battle was won by the 2,936 airmen he called 'The Few'. In his words, 'Never in the field of conflict was so much owed by so many to so few.' This monument is to their glorious memory.

This book, also written and published in honour of 'The Few', gives a fascinating insight into the background and events, the machines and men of that extraordinary time. It is a worthy companion to the Monument.

THE BATTLE OF BRITAIN MONUMENT

There can be no better tribute to the 'Few' than Paul Day's outstanding Monument on London's Embankment. Here, the artist tells the story behind his exceptional work

From the outset the form of the Monument was dictated by the nature of the available space, and by planning constraints along the Embankment. When I first walked along the river between Westminster and Hungerford bridges my ideas about the future Monument were, unbeknown to me, in harmony with these practical restrictions. I observed a panorama of major architectural landmarks on a grand scale: the Palace of Westminster, the former GLC building, the Ministry of Defence headquarters and the London Eye. The river walk is also awash with various sculpted monuments that look great from a distance but that do not really bear close inspection. I decided what was needed was something on a human scale that would offer the passer-by something rich in detail when seen up close, and not just another monolith to be admired from afar, of which there are plenty already. The existing plinth, being low and long, would serve my purposes precisely. It could be used as a wall on which to tell the tale of the Battle of Britain with a sculpted storyboard in high relief and which would present itself to the viewer at eye-level, thus being accessible to all ages and intimate rather than grand and distant. Commissioned to produce the Monument, much to my delight, I met Tony Dyson, the architect, who shared my interpretation of the site, and who would enrich my original thoughts with his own clear-sightedness.

I proceeded to research the subject as thoroughly as possible and during a three month period did nothing but read books, watch films and interview veterans, with a view to being totally immersed in the Battle of Britain. Of course, encountering the veterans meant not only hearing of the extraordinary feats of courage first hand from ex-pilots and gunners, but those other veterans, the aircraft themselves, spoke volumes about the exhilaration and physical challenge of 1940's air combat. The chance to fly with my RAF namesake and Squadron Leader of the Battle of Britain Memorial Flight was too good an opportunity to miss. An hour in the air with Sqn Ldr Paul Day brought home to me with force just how physically trying it was to sustain hard manoeuvring in the air, albeit without the cannon shells flying around my ears.

The Monument is made up of two relief panels facing in opposite directions. On the one I wished to commemorate the unique achievement of Fighter Command and give the entire space over to telling their story. On the other I wanted to portray something of the wider experience, of the nation as a whole at war. The few thousand pilots, gunners, ground crews and WAAFs are undoubtedly the heroes of the hour, but I felt it important for future generations to remember the other countless acts of self sacrifice and heroism among the British people, without which the RAF could not so well have defended the nation.

I feel it important to add that my desire has been to create a work of contemporary art and not to adopt the manners of a previous period or style which has so often been the case with public monuments in the past. Conservativism is not the best way to give life to an historic subject in art. The work has to take on a life of its own if it is to speak now and to future generations and not to look 'past it' from the beginning. The Battle of Britain is an epic moment in history, but one of modernity where the latest air technology was vital. The Monument is not the representation of a tomb where hundreds of thousands lie dead. It is the celebration of excellent organisation, youthful enthusiasm, devotion to duty, and national unity. I hope it will remind future generations of the hardship that was endured by our grandparents to defend the British people and their traditions, which could so nearly have been lost to fascism.

FIRST PANEL – FIGHTER COMMAND

PILOTS AT REST

Waiting for the signal to be brought to 'readiness' or to 'scramble' (take off) allowed the pilots much needed time to rest. The backdrop of the English Channel is a reminder of where too many pilots were to end up finding a place of permanent rest. WAAFs crop up at different intervals, looking down, and watching over, their pilots. I see them as guardian angels, willing their young men home to safety or to a pain-free end.

THE OBSERVERS

Scattered around the coast and inland, the 30,000-strong Observer Corps ceaselessly scoured the air to intercept, visually and orally, enemy raiders. After RDF (Radio Direction Finding, later known as radar) volunteer observers were the next line of intelligence, relaying crucial information to Group and Sector Stations.

MECHANICS AND RIGGERS

None praise the work of the ground crews more highly than pilots themselves, whose very lives depended on the vigilance and efficiency of their RAF colleagues. Their tasks were more repetitive, their heroism less glamorous than that of the aircrews, but they shared significantly in the danger and took many risks. From bombing raids to machine gun sweeps by enemy fighters, the ground crews faced battle at the sharp end. Here the armourers wrestle with bullet belts whilst arming Hurricane fighters.

'SCRAMBLE'

That classic moment, when the signal to 'scramble' is given, *had* to take centre stage. It is the very symbol of the Battle. In this case, the pilots surge off the wall, out of their picture and onto the pavement, into our world, a reminder that these men really did exist and do those incredible things.

PILOT'S HEAD AND PLOTTERS

Depicting an air battle in painting or sculpture is never easy. Aviation painting generally adopts the viewpoint of a fixed lens attached to the wing of an observation aircraft, maintained at reasonable distance from the action to serve the needs of composition. The image is normally taken at a thousandth of a second and completely freezes the action. I adopted the view that air combat took place above all in the cockpit and in the eye of the combatant, that it was fast and somewhat blurred. It is as much about the psychological intensity etched into the pilot's brow as the superb ellipses described by a Supermarine Spitfire trying to avoid a pursuing Messerschmitt Me 109. In this case, with the huge pilot's head, I wanted to put us in touch with the flesh and blood behind the machine, though in some way, the flesh and blood and the machine are one. A young face can look old when enduring excessive physical danger and intense concentration. This I hope is the case with this pilot who is surrounded by speed, smoke and tracer fire. He is not alone, however. His moves are being followed; his sometimes frantic speech passes directly from the air into the ears of the young girls at the plotting tables who will him on to victory and home to safety, who may even share his last moments of agony.

TALES FROM THE MESS

Young, inexperienced pilots drank in the commentaries of their battle-hardened counterparts. Knowledge gained this way was as necessary to their survival as the initial flying course. I imagine that it was camaraderie and a sense of the squadron spirit that gave those young men the strength to face death and injury on a more or less daily basis. Having read a great many pilots' memoirs, I am still amazed at how easily death came through accident and inexperience: a raised undercarriage on landing, navigational error, or unchecked propeller pitch.

SECOND PANEL – BRITAIN AT WAR

SLIT TRENCH

There are some superb archive photographs of Kentish hop pickers watching from the shelter of slit trenches, the air battle raging overhead. The expression on many faces seems, at this early stage of the war at least, to be one of curiosity and fascination. The real nature of the threat had not yet become apparent. Images of London's children sheltering in the same way reveal their amusement at seeing tracer dots racing around the skies. Not exactly what I imagine when thinking of the front line of a war. Yet this was Britain in 1940. The contrast between civilian normality and a pilot's life at 'angels twenty' was marked.

GUNNERS

The threat appears in the form of aerial bombardment. At first only the RAF installations were targeted. Illusions of a clean war remained intact, that is before civilian casualty statistics started to rocket. The gunners pass shells from one to the other before their ultimate discharge into the sky. Before researching the Monument I had no idea how anti-aircraft shells worked, that the art was in choosing the correctly timed fuse, as well as in accurate aim. In the kiss blown between the gunner and a factory girl I want to remind us that this action did not take place in some sort of heroic bubble, but in a world of human feeling and frailty. Time, in removing events and their witnesses from us, seems to filter out most of what is common in human experience, making it seem distant and unreal. Anecdotal humour can perhaps remedy slightly this distortion of time.

THE ROLE OF WOMEN

Liberation for women: this war wrote a major chapter in the evolution of society's attitude to women at work in the war. The woman worker's role did not stop at the aircraft and munitions factory gates. Women ferry pilots also delivered new combat aircraft from factory to airfield. This is not political correctness, just interesting, historical fact.

DOGFIGHT

In my mind, pilots have to be at the centre of this Monument on both sides. Their lives are at its heart. As I wrote earlier, I have chosen to portray a pilot's eye view of air combat and not that of the aviation painter. In any case, skies in relief sculpture are not the easiest of subjects to convey. I have put the head of a Messerschmitt pilot onto the shoulder of an RAF one, to try and create the sense of a duel being fought out by two knights of the air, in close proximity and to the death. The 'Hun in the Sun' has the advantage, but as their aircraft fly past behind them, the Spitfire has managed to slip onto the tail of the Me 109 and has caught it with tracer fire. The pilots on both sides had a healthy respect one for the other. Likewise, in this work, I am in admiration of all the young men who took part.

ST PAUL'S CATHEDRAL

St Paul's became the symbol of resistance during the Blitz having remained standing while all around was seemingly demolished. The famous news photo collage of the Cathedral inspired this sequence. Although, not part of the Battle of Britain as such, the Blitz was the direct result of Dowding's successful strategy to save the RAF and keep fighters in the air at all costs. German attack passed from airfields and factories to almost any other legitimate and less legitimate target.

SEARCHING THE RUINS

I think one of the most harrowing aspects of the Battle of Britain was bombing of heavily populated areas, using inaccurate means, and the subsequent horrors that befell certain cities. The suddenness of loss through bombardment is dramatically portrayed in Guy Hamilton's film version, *The Battle of Britain* (1969). That people could wake up the morning after a bombardment and find their home blown away is terrifying. Of course, some were never to wake up at all. This scene is in homage to the rescue services and a reminder that, although the British people were tried by fire, the nation was never to be put through occupation and the trauma that entailed. In any case, had we lost this battle, the war in Europe would have been irrevocably lost.

'BREW UP'

Making tea in an 'Anderson' shelter is not an act of great heroism, more one of defiance. I like this as an image of the British spirit of 1940 – like the home guard armed with broom handles and supplied with bicycles; the removal of signposts to confound enemy invaders; the collection of saucepans for the war effort; a tin dug-out at the bottom of an ordinary garden, offering shelter to a suburban family against 1000-pounders. Perhaps derisory means on the face of it, but cultivating that immensely powerful spirit of resistance so essential to the nation's survival.

A MONUMENTAL TASK

Tony Dyson, architect, reveals the story behind the commission and construction of the Monument

It was back in August 2000 that Bill Bond of the Battle of Britain Historical Society approached us about the Society's project for a monument to the Battle of Britain in London. Bill had been lobbying Westminster City Council for an appropriate site for some time and at last, at the suggestion of English Heritage, the Council had come up with a potential site on the Victoria Embankment: between the statue of Boadicea, in the shadow of Big Ben, to the south and the RAF Memorial mid-way between Hungerford and Westminster Bridges, to the north. The site was also near the memorials to The Fleet Air Arm, Viscount Trenchard, 'Father of the Royal Air Force' and Viscount Portal, Marshal of the Royal Air Force – all in Victoria Embankment Gardens, in front of the Ministry of Defence.

Westminster City Council had told Bill Bond that the Historical Society would need an architect to guide them through the complicated planning process and deal with design and constructional matters. Over the following five years, our role developed into that of Project Manager, dealing with many other aspects of the project.

The site consisted of a 25m long, 2m wide and 2m high granite structure, clearly – from its architectural detailing –

part of Bazalgette's original Embankment works and rumoured to be the top of a flue incorporated to ventilate the smoke from the steam trains of the underground railway constructed beneath the road nearby. Initial enquiries as to who owned the structure drew a blank – Westminster City Council said it was London Underground, London Underground said it did not appear on their deeds and an application to the Land Registry revealed that the Embankment had never been officially registered when it had been built out over the Thames river banks in the 19th century! London Underground Limited was eventually persuaded to agree to own the structure, so that the completed Monument could be given to Westminster City Council for maintenance in perpetuity.

One of the Battle of Britain Historical Society's original requirements had been that the monument should list the names of all the 2936 pilots and aircrew who flew in the Battle of Britain between 10 July and 31 October 1940. Although the extreme length of the granite structure made it suitable for this purpose, it was difficult to see how a sculptural element might be incorporated. There had been a proliferation of monuments of varying quality in the City of

Westminster in recent years and, as a result, schemes for monuments submitted for planning and Listed Building consents needed to be commented on by Westminster City Council's Public Art Advisory Panel. This body, along with English Heritage, would require the Monument to be a first rate example of public art, and worthy of such a prominent site in the Capital.

In order to develop the design and find a suitable sculptor we organised a limited competition, appointing a Selection Committee consisting of Sir Jeremy Isaacs, television director and producer (*The World At War*); Robin Simon FSA, Editor, British Art Journal, Arts Editor, Daily Mail; Bill Bond, Founder and Chief Executive of the Battle of Britain Historical Society; Air Commodore Peter Brothers CBE, DSO, DFC & Bar; and myself as Chairman.

Using the resources of the Royal Society of British Sculptors and in particular the maquette library at Sculpture at Goodwood, I formed a list of 20 or so potential sculptors which, with the help of Committee members, I whittled down to six, all of whom had exhibited quite different approaches in their previous work. One then dropped out because of pressure of work and the final list became Paul Day, Charlotte Mayer, Michael Sandle, Alexander Stoddart and Almuth Tebbenhoff. I then wrote a brief, which I tried to keep as open as possible, and all competitors were invited to show their ideas in the form of a maquette (model), for a nominal fee, presenting them to the Selection Committee in Sculpture at Goodwood's gallery in Sussex, on 23 February 2002. This resulted in two sculptors being short listed. Further consultation with Westminster City Council led to the choice of Paul Day, whose approach allowed us to exploit the extreme 25m length of the structure, without challenging the vertical dominance of the RAF Memorial. Paul's extraordinary ability to communicate detailed information in his reliefs also fulfilled the Historical Society's requirement that the Monument should educate people about the Battle of Britain whilst creating a remarkable and unique work of art of the highest quality.

Paul's scheme consisted of two bronze reliefs, one facing the Thames and the other facing the road, with a bust of an airman raised high on a pedestal between. On the reverse sides of the reliefs were lists of the pilots' and air crews'

names. Developing these ideas we proposed cutting a walkway through the structure, but on the diagonal and in the direction of the monuments in front of the Ministry of Defence, so that Paul's bronze reliefs could be experienced together, first on one side of the walkway and then on the other, the reliefs being connected across the gap in the centre by a large RAF Roundel in the paving pattern. Bronze plaques – with the names of the pilots and aircrew raised against back-plates engraved with line drawings of the aircraft involved – would then be wrapped around the outside of the Monument, the openings in the walls being bordered by the badges of the Squadrons. At the end facing the RAF Memorial there would be a large bronze badge of RAF Fighter Command. One in six of the pilots and aircrew

were from countries outside the United Kingdom and so, to show this, we proposed that the names on the plaques be grouped according to the airmen's country of origin.

It was this scheme which we presented to Westminster City Council's Public Art Advisory Panel, and received a favourable response. The Historical Society then appointed Maurice Djanogly to mastermind the fundraising for the project. With previous projects, Maurice had raised a considerable proportion of the funds needed by selling maquettes of the sculpture. In our case, the concept of bronze reliefs, rather than a single sculpture symbolising the subject of the memorial, posed a potential problem. To solve this Paul Day came up with the image of a group of pilots scrambling for their aircraft which, after considering a number of

alternative positions, we incorporated into the centre of the bronze relief facing the road where we felt it would provide a focus for ceremonial purposes whilst still maintaining the flow of interest across the overall sculptural composition.

A second presentation to show these material changes in the design to the Public Art Advisory Panel drew a negative response and the comment that a more abstract approach might be more appropriate. Undaunted, (and remembering Winston Churchill's famous abbreviation KBO!) we pressed on with our design and in preparation for our submissions for both planning and Listed Building consents, liaised with the following: The Environment Agency because the site was near the river wall, which acted as a flood barrier and so the works would need a separate permission from the Agency; London Underground Limited and Transport for London because the structure at the heart of the Monument was not only a former vent to the Circle and District Lines but lay on the border between pavements under the jurisdiction of the City of Westminster and Transport for London; the various Departments of Westminster City Council that would be involved; English Heritage and others who would be consulted under the applications. The Historical Society then appointed Brian Lawrence of Bucknall Austin as quantity surveyor for the project and professor R. Narayanan as the structural engineer, who also became involved with the digging of trial holes and other site investigations.

Marian Ferriday organised the project's press launch and continued to deal with press and publicity throughout the project. We achieved our planning and Listed Building Consents in January 2004, going out to tender later that year to four contractors, the contract being won by Stonewest.

While Paul Day was producing his clay models for the bronze reliefs, we began to progress our detailed designs for the 28 large bronze plaques surrounding the Monument. We started with the difficult task of establishing an accurate list of the names of the pilots and aircrew who flew in the Battle, this problem only being solved once The Historical Society's Edward McManus became involved. Our graphic designer Ann Humphrey coordinated the layouts of the lettering of the names with the designs for the engravings on the back-plates of the plaques, all in a computer program to suit the machines of the foundry's pattern maker and backed up by a team of computer technicians, some of whom went on later to produce the detailed drawings for the construction phase.

Once Paul Day's bronze reliefs had been cast by the Morris Singer Foundry, we were able to carry out further lighting trials and develop the design of the fibre optic lighting systems with Light Projects and Light Matters and the stainless steel lighting canopies and bollards that would contain them, with Woodhouse. Stonewest started on site in January 2005, three weeks later than programmed because of a lack of communication between officers in Transport for London and Westminster City Council (separate permissions had to be obtained from each organisation for the pavement works). Parts of the granite structure were dismantled and taken down to the De Lank quarry in Cornwall to be cut up prior to rebuilding as plinths for the bronze reliefs and new granite for the new roof, to match the existing granite, was supplied by Fyfe Glenrock in Aberdeenshire. After a dramatic craning in of both of the bronze reliefs, each weighing two tons, Stonewest completed the works shortly before the unveiling on the 18 September 2005.

EQUAL TO THE CALL

Per Ardua ad Astra

MOTTO OF THE ROYAL AIR FORCE

The Royal Air Force had prepared to fight the Battle of Britain long before the Second World War began. Their adversaries had not. It was the conflict a nation at arms had expected, after Germany walked out of the Disarmament Conference, and the League of Nations, in 1933.

News from British agents in Germany that the National Socialists were rearming in violation of the Versailles Treaty, aiming for supremacy of the skies by building a clandestine air force, led to a British Cabinet decision to increase the Home Defence Air Force. In 1935, expansion was hastened by the announcement at a conference between Adolf Hitler and Sir John Simon, the Foreign Secretary, that German air parity with Britain had already been reached. A force equal to that of Britain and France was the Nazi dictator's next objective.

A succession of Cabinet approved rearmament schemes – with emphasis on double priority for bombers over fighters – echoed the pre-war dread of bombing against great cities in an atmosphere of international threat and counter threat. A fear summarised in Stanley Baldwin's speech to the House of Commons in 1932 that 'the bomber will always get through.'

Baldwin was accused by sections of the press of being an alarmist, but in 1934, when 70 per cent of attacking planes in air exercises over London reached their targets, he delivered himself of the opinion that 'Since the days of the air the old frontiers are gone. When you think of the defence of England, you no longer think of the chalk cliffs of Dover, you think of the Rhine. That is where our frontier lies.' Some newspapers criticized Baldwin for suggesting that Germany might be the enemy.

In the same year, Winston Churchill spoke out in the House of Commons against the strongest aircraft industry in Europe: 'Germany is rearming on land; she is rearming also to some extent at sea; but what concerns us most of all is the rearmament of Germany in the air.' Churchill, denied office by Baldwin and 'in the wilderness',

OPPOSITE *Defence of the Realm*: Spitfires of 54 Squadron line up at Hornchurch Sector Station during the final Home Defence Exercises, August 1939. A month later the nation was at war.

forecast that 'two years from now…the German air force will be nearly 50 per cent stronger (than our own), and in 1937 nearly double. All this is on the assumption that there is no acceleration on the part of Germany, and no slowing down on our part…Beware: Germany is a country fertile in military surprises!'

Baldwin responded for the government: 'Such investigations as I have been able to make lead me to believe that the right honourable member for Epping's figures are considerably exaggerated.' The Conservative *Daily Telegraph*, in support of the Prime Minister, reported that 'Eleven new sites for aerodromes have been selected, six have been acquired; plans for altering some forty of the older stations are in hand; one new training school for flying has been opened and another will be ready in April.'

Air Commodore Douglas Evill, visiting Berlin in 1936 as a guest of the Luftwaffe, reported:

The final conclusion is that within twelve months the Germans will have strong and highly organized air defences, and a large and well-equipped air force which would be very difficult to destroy if that were to prove necessary. An impression is given that, if only for professional reasons, they would even then prefer to have further time to consolidate this force before putting it into operation. Whether they have the resources to do so and the political stability to proceed for several years at the present pace is beyond comment in this paper, but, if the answer is yes, it is impossible to avoid the conclusion that Germany in 1940 will possess a thoroughly well-organised air force of high efficiency and morale.

Rearmament made war more likely and support for the coming age of the long-range heavy bomber reflected the commonly held RAF view that offensive strategy – represented by a 'knock out blow' from bomber fleets – would prove to be a war-winning weapon. Indeed, Lord Trenchard, the first chief of Air Staff, whose influence in the formative years of the RAF was absolute, was convinced fighters were no match for bomber squadrons.

Yet, notably, in 1937, pursuit of parity with Germany's bomber force by the Air Ministry and the RAF was halted by Sir Thomas Inskip. The minister in charge of defence co-ordination, Inskip dismissed the latest rearmament scheme as too costly, and demanded higher priority for fighter production. Fighters were cheaper to build than bombers, and Inskip was bent on economy. However, he justified his proposal on strategic grounds: 'I cannot take the view' he wrote, 'that our Air Force must necessarily correspond to number and type of aircraft with the German Air Force.' A strong fighter arm, he argued, could defend the country should attack come. 'The role of our Air Force is not an early knock-out blow – no one has suggested that we can accomplish that – but to prevent the Germans from knocking us out.'

ABOVE *Bomber force*: King George VI inspects the Bristol 130 prototype, RAF Martlesham Heath, July 1936. The Armstrong-Whitworth prototype bomber transport behind was developed as the Whitley. Bomber Command was assigned a crucial complementary role during the battle.

The Cabinet backed Inskip, finally approving a revised plan acknowledging the requirement for more front-line fighters. The acceptance of Inskip's proposal for a heightened fighter presence was one more factor in shifting emphasis from the efficacy of a bomber offensive to the merits of fighter defence. The star of the fighter aircraft was in the ascendant.

One man who tried to raise the alarm over Winston Churchill's 'corridor of deepening and darkening danger' was Air Chief Marshal Sir Hugh Dowding, Commander-in-Chief, Fighter Command, on its foundation in 1936:

> The best defence of the country is the fear of the fighter. If we were strong in fighters we should probably never be attacked in force. If we are moderately strong we shall probably be attacked and the attacks will gradually be brought to a standstill... If we are weak in fighter strength, the attacks will not be brought to a standstill and the productive capacity of the country will be virtually destroyed.

Major General E.B.Ashmore, commanding London's air defences in World War One, acknowledged that fighters were the first means of defence, but strongly advocated a

system of control from the ground. Ashmore set up a central control, comprising a large map fixed on a table, round which 'plotters' wearing headphones took instructions. Ashmore, writing in 1918, recalled:

> I sat overlooking the map from the raised gallery; in effect, I could follow the course of all aircraft flying over the country, as the counters crept across the map. The system worked very rapidly. From the time when an observer at one of the stations in the country saw a machine over him, to the time when the counter representing it appeared on my map, was not, as a rule, more than half a minute. By my side, in the gallery, sat the air forced commander... with direct command lines to his squadrons, and a special line to a long-range wireless transmitter at Biggin Hill. This transmitter was used for giving orders to leaders of defending formations in the air during day time, in accordance with the movements of the enemy as shown on the control map.

By 1936 the former area organization of the Air Defence of Great Britain (ADGB) had been replaced by functional commands: Fighter, Bomber, Coastal, Training, and later Maintenance Command. At Fighter Command headquarters Bentley Priory, a late eighteenth century gothic mansion in Stanmore on the outskirts of London, Dowding refined the principles of Ashmore's system. He showed much firmness of purpose in creating a formidable fighter force for what he foresaw as his command's historic mission: the defence of the realm.

The appointment of Dowding by the Air Ministry proved an inspired move. A reserve officer in the Royal Flying Corps who had learned to fly at Brooklands, he saw service during the First World War, commanding a wing in France, and specialised in the use of wireless communication from the air. A career airman, Dowding organized several post-war RAF pageants at Hendon. In 1930 he was made Air Member for the new department of Research and Development, in a climate where officers with progressive scientific ideas were being sidelined by the War Office. Research and development was generally neglected in an epoch characterised by unprecedented peacetime investment in air stations – over 50 permanent stations were constructed between 1923 and 1939 – and overmanning at the Air Ministry.

Hugh 'Cocky' Dundas, who celebrated his 20th birthday as a Battle of Britain pilot, was to recall:

> The importance of Dowding's personal role in preparing for the Battle of Britain and carrying it through to a successful conclusion cannot be overestimated. To 'Stuffy' Dowding (a nickname his austere and withdrawn manner had earned for him) the squadrons were all that mattered and nothing was too good for his pilots. To get them what they needed he would, and did, go to any lengths, fight

OPPOSITE *Leader of the 'Few'*: Air Chief Marshal Sir Hugh Dowding, head of Fighter Command. His determination to limit the number of fighters sent to France was one of the vitally correct decisions of the war.

LEFT *Bentley Priory*: Dowding's office (in restored form) at Fighter Command headquarters, Stanmore, Middlesex. Dowding was replaced after the battle, a decision that has been open to debate ever since. He was created Baron Dowding of Bentley Priory in 1943.

any opposition, gladly risk the displeasure of the highest and most powerful. 'Stuffy' was not a word of contempt, but rather of affection.

W.G.G. Duncan-Smith, another leading airman in the battle, wrote in his memoirs that Dowding had 'schemed the victory', ranking his former chief 'an all-time great among the commanders.' General Sir Frederick Pile, wartime head of Anti-Aircraft Command, who met Dowding daily during the battle and widely admired Fighter Command's C-in-C, wrote: 'A most difficult man, a self-opinionated man, a most determined man, and a man who knew more than anybody about all aspects of aerial warfare.'

Dowding's scheme for effective close air defence hinged on two key elements: early detection of the approach of hostile aircraft, to give his pilots the best chance of striking at massed bomber fleets before they hit their targets; and squadrons of high performance, low-wing cantilever monoplane fighters, equipped with superior hitting power.

A new age of record-breaking on land, sea and in the air began during the Twenties,

BELOW LEFT *No new thing:* RAF Gloster biplanes take to the skies. Formation flying and aerobatic displays were popularised by the annual Hendon Air Pageant between the wars.

BELOW RIGHT *Twin wings:* 56 Squadron Gladiators in a simulated alarm, North Weald, August 1937. The white 'Sidcot' suits worn were designed by a pilot, Sidney Cotton. Demands for an airframe capable of greater and greater speed led to the eclipse of the biplane.

and the success of R.J. Mitchell's streamlined Supermarine floatplanes in the series of bi-annual Schneider Trophy races – won outright for Britain in 1931 – set the scene for a new generation of fighters taking to the skies. The S.6B seaplane built at the Supermarine Aviation works at Eastleigh near Southampton, and powered by a Rolls-Royce 'R' type engine, ultimately took the world air speed record to 407mph, using special chemical fuels.

Hugh Dundas, who became chief defence correspondent of the *Evening Standard*, later wrote:

> Dowding recognized that the performances of these extraordinary airplanes represented a break through which had an application for the RAF and particularly for fighter airplanes. At a time when all the world was concentrating on the further development of super manoeuvrable biplane fighters his mind took the big step forward. He called for a low wing monoplane fighter, with retractable undercarriage, enclosed cockpit and guns, mounted in the wings. There were many traditionalists who were entirely opposed to the whole conception. And when Dowding later insisted that the number of guns should be increased to eight he was accused of taking leave of his senses. But what he had produced was in fact the specification for the Hurricane and Spitfire.

In a period of rapid technical development in aircraft technology, those traditionalists stuck to the outmoded wood and canvas biplane, all struts and wires. Monoplanes were reckoned by some members of the old guard to be 'un-English'. As late as the Spanish Civil War in 1937, the British air attaché in Paris rated manoeuvrability above speed. The Battle of Britain, altering air combat out of all recognition, would prove him wrong.

Nothing less than the Hurricane and the Spitfire could successfully oppose the menace of the Luftwaffe's air armada in 1940.

Absurdly enough but in typically British fashion, it was a sporting event which had an enormous influence upon aircraft development in Britain. A Frenchman, M. Schneider, had in 1913 presented a trophy, to be competed for annually, for the fastest seaplane. Various seaplane manufacturers began to take an interest in this competition and in 1914 the first race was flown. It was won by Britain... At one time it looked as though we should not be able to compete in 1931 owing to government apathy and Treasury economy. However, a private person, Lady Houston, came forward with the necessary cash and, in combination, Messrs Vickers Supermarine and Messrs Rolls-Royce produced the winning aircraft and engine. This machine was the forerunner of the Spitfire...

SIR PHILIP JOUBERT DE LA FERTÉ,
THE THIRD SERVICE

THE MAGIC EYE OF RADAR

Scientists made a spectacular contribution to winning the Second World War. One of their most remarkable achievements was the work done on Radio Direction Finding ('RDF'), based on the discovery that aircraft interfered with radio beams, and better known as radar (radio detecting and ranging).

Perhaps no one in the RAF between the wars was better informed about the potential of scientific research than Dowding, who had directed the technical progress of the service in his role as Air Member responsible for Research and Development. One of his biographers referred to radar as the 'Oracle of Fighter Command.'

Dowding realised that standing patrols covering all threatened areas, including shipping, were costly and impracticable. Yet early warning and continuous observation, and approximation of range, direction, strength and height of the oncoming enemy attack was essential if pilots were to be ordered off the ground at the right time to intercept a raid before reaching its objective. The use of sound-detectors, and later 'acoustical mirrors' in the form of giant curved concrete rectangles, sited on England's south coast, was limited by range and general interference.

It is experiment and verification that occupies scientists and, in 1934, the Committee for the Scientific Survey of Air Defence was formed, including two scientists from Dowding's department – H.E. Wimperis, Director of Scientific Research, and his assistant A.P. Rowe, acting as secretary – and Sir Henry Tizard, the most distinguished scientific civil servant of his generation. The small group, led by Tizard, a former pilot who worked closely with a far from uncritical Dowding, was chiefly responsible for bringing into being a radar network crucial to the defence of Britain in 1940.

The committee circulated research establishments such as the Radio Research section at the National Physical Laboratory, run by the outstanding Scottish scientist Robert (later Sir Robert) Watson-Watt. Rumours of a 'death ray' – a beam with huge radiant power capable of downing aircraft – was instantly dismissed, but Watson-Watt drafted

'Well, then, if the death ray is not possible, how can we help them?'

ROBERT WATSON-WATT

OPPOSITE *Flying start*: 602 Squadron Spitfire over Firth of Forth. If fighters were to have a chance of intercepting the enemy before he dropped his bombs, they had to be alerted when the intruders were still out to sea.

ABOVE *The right direction*: Robert Watson-Watt, Scottish-born scientist and leading advocate of radar. He considered Dowding to be unreceptive to new ideas.

OPPOSITE *Early warning*: no concerted effort was made to black-out radar targets. The lattice structures required almost a direct hit to knock them down. One of the Luftwaffe's major errors was to underrate the range and effectiveness of radar.

a proposal for using radio beams to pick up aircraft: *The Detection of Aircraft by Radio Methods*. Hugh Dundas wrote that 'the sum of ten thousand pounds was needed for further experiments. Dowding immediately grasped the vast significance of Watson-Watt's claims but cannily insisted on realistic field trials before asking for the money.'

The Tizard committee, risking all on the development of radar, invited Watson-Watt to demonstrate his theories. On 26 February 1935, Watson-Watt and Rowe were parked in a converted ambulance in a field in the Northamptnshire village of Weedon. Inside was a receiver with a cathode-ray oscillograph attached; outside was an aerial system of cables mounted on poles across the grass; above droned a RAF Heyford bomber.

Squadron Leader R.S.Blucke dutifully flew the bomber up and down a fixed line corresponding to the lateral centre of a transmitted beam via the local BBC radio station at Daventry. The demonstration confirmed that the aircraft interfered with the radio waves, radiating a signal registered on the screen as a 'blip'. Blucke's bomber had been tracked southwards, at 10,000 feet, for about eight miles.

Rowe passed the results to Wimperis, who reported to Dowding that 'We now have in embryo, a new and potent means of detecting the approach of hostile aircraft, one which will be independent of mist, cloud, fog or nightfall.' A keen sense of the potential for increasing the vulnerability of attacking aircraft convinced Tizard and his colleagues that Watson-Watt's pioneering work was, quoting Dowding, 'a discovery of the highest importance'. Watson-Watt was at once requested to submit proposals for an under cover 'RDF' system. The Treasury granted the money for development, and the search was on for a site for a radio research station, found at the former home of the Air Ministry Experimental Flying Section at Orfordness.

On a bleak strip of Suffolk coastline, laboratories and workshops were constructed, and transmission and receiving aerials erected. The air base at nearby Martlesham Heath provided flights for the early transmitter and receiver trials, and by September aircraft were being detected at a range of 50 miles. Tower and aerial designs were approved, and the Air Defence Sub-Committee recommended construction of a chain of radar-stations covering the southern and eastern coasts from the Isle of Wight to Dundee.

Watson-Watt and his team, crowded out of the Orfordness site, moved to Bawdsey Manor, an imposing Victorian house close to the Deben estuary, Suffolk in March 1936.

Bawdsey, the first of the Chain Home radar-stations, ringed by a series of concrete pillboxes on the landward side, was dwarfed by four high-standing lattice masts, permitting the transmission of long wavelength signals.

The build-up and pace of activity under the shadow of war was unrelenting. In an atmosphere similar to that of an English country house weekend, scientists and engineers, visiting politicians and RAF officers were encouraged to exchange ideas, and contradict one another if they thought they were wrong, in unsparing debates known as Bawdsey 'Soviets'. Construction of the chain of transmitter-receiver stations – called AMES (Air Ministry Experimental Stations) – was conducted under tight security, yet the soaring towers, facing seawards, were clearly visible from the French coast.

In 1938, under the spur of Sir Henry Tizard, the RAF fighter station at Biggin Hill was used as the all-important testing ground for fighter direction exercises, linking radar to the intercepting aircraft under operational conditions. The 'Biggin Hill Experiment' used ground controllers and plotting tables, and a converging course reckoning dubbed the 'Tizzy angle.' By August 1939, when the swastika-bearing *Graf Zeppelin* airship flew over Britain's north-east coast in a thwarted effort to pick up signals, 20 Chain Home (CH) stations circled Britain's coastline. Operators of the cathode-ray tubes in the 'receiver hut' at the base of the twin sets of transmitter (350 feet) and receiver (240 feet) towers could detect aircraft at a range of 100 miles, theoretically giving the bearing, height and number of the approaching formation. A system of Chain Home Low (CHL) stations with rotating aerials, chiefly the work of Australian scientist W.A.S.Butement, was built after the outbreak of war to pick up raiders below 3,000 feet, and coastal shipping.

By June 1940, with the Battle of Britain very close, Fighter Command aircraft were equipped with IFF (Identification Friend or Foe), a small transmitting device that operated within British radar range, and distinguished between friendly and hostile aircraft on the radar screen. Pilots automatically reported their positions by using another device, 'Pip-Squeak', and a Very High Frequency (VHF) radio-telephone provided clear, direct speech between the operations room and the air.

The successful interception of raids in the Battle of Britain was not always easy, but when the test came, radar dominated the aerial battle, offering Fighter Command's pilots a level of performance of a different order. It was a brilliant achievement.

TOUCHING THE HEIGHTS

The Hurricane and the Spitfire, household names, have entered the Battle of Britain pantheon. The once familiar exhaust note of the Rolls-Royce Merlin-powered combat aircraft became the sound of the RAF in battle in 1940. Even today, when a lone Hurricane or Spitfire is overhead, the sight can still generate a sense of awe and romance. But the aura is due to more than just appearance. Like all great engineering projects, the high-speed fighter embodied a dream: the intercepting fighter as part of a scientific structure of air defence to hold the thin blue line of battle at home.

Rolls-Royce powered the Supermarine seaplane to outright victory in the 1931 Schneider Trophy and in a brief span of years developed 'a pilot's engine' to meet the needs of both Fighter and Bomber Command. Ernest Hives, Rolls-Royce Works General Manager, was responsible for delivering the PV XII (PV denoted 'Private Venture') derived from the successful Kestrel engine, and later known as the Merlin. The Merlin's destiny was irrevocably linked to the Battle of Britain, and the high boost, liquid-cooled 12-cylinder design was *the* major combat engine in a straight-out aerial fight that changed the mood of war in the air. The pressure to keep one jump ahead of a determined adversary saw Hives push the engine build programme ahead of Air Ministry expectations.

The Hawker Hurricane came first. Like the Vickers Supermarine Spitfire, the outcome of the decision of the Air Staff, influenced by Dowding, to circulate among private manufacturers a specification for a front line fighter with a maximum speed of more than 300 mph, and an armament of eight machine-guns.

At the Air Ministry Squadron Leader Ralph Sorley, posted to the Operational Requirements branch, became sharply aware of the culture of aggression that was taking over the German psyche with the advent of Hitler and Nazism. Sorley was convinced that sooner or later there would be a war, and his contribution to the development of fighter armament cannot be over-emphasized. He noted, significantly, that an intense rate of fire was demanded to shoot down enemy bombers:

> *Flying a Spitfire was rather like being a kid and being asked to drive a Bugatti with somebody else paying for the fuel.*
>
> TOM NEIL

OPPOSITE *Squadron Spitfires at Sawbridgeworth, Herts* by Eric Ravilious (1903-1942). A painter, graphic artist, designer and Official War Artist, Ravilious failed to return when his plane went 'missing' over Iceland.

By dint of much blotting paper, arithmetic and burning of midnight oil, I reached the answer of eight guns as being the number required to give a lethal dose in two seconds of fire. I reckoned that the bomber's speed would probably be such as to allow the pursuing fighter only one chance of attack so it must be destroyed in that vital two-second burst.

In 1940 Hurricane and Spitfire squadrons entered the Battle of Britain equipped with a peak of striking power in the form of eight .303 Browning machine guns, four in each wing set to fire forward outside the airscrew disc.

BELOW *Into battle*: Hawker Hurricane, 32 Squadron, Hawkinge. 'Simply and robustly built' said Bob Foster, 605 Squadron, 'she could absorb as well as hand out punishment, and we had an implicit faith in her ability to get us home.'

The highest praise is reserved for Sydney Camm, the pragmatic chief designer at Hawker, who made his name with the Hart and Fury biplanes. The Hurricane was Camm's answer to the latest Air Ministry specification calling for the mounting of eight machine guns. Camm's robust design used existing Hawker tools and jigs to save costs, and the closely-aligned battery of eight Brownings supplied real hitting power. Originally constructed of wood and fabric for ease of build and repair, the Hurricane was strengthened by a frame of tubular steel and duralumin. A wide inward-folding retractable undercarriage proved a capital advantage on rough airfield surfaces during the Battle of Britain and after.

The prototype K5083 first flew at Brooklands, 'the cradle of aviation', on 6 November 1935, piloted by 'George' Bulman. On landing Hawker's chief test pilot announced that the test flight had been 'a piece of cake'. Camm's successful single-wing design was an historic example of a fighter that reached production due to the entrepreneurial spirit of a private manufacturer. The directors of Hawker authorised production of 1,000 Hurricanes ahead of the Air Ministry order for 600 (plus 310 Spitfires) in June 1936.

The Mark I Hurricane was first delivered to 111 Squadron at Northolt in January 1938. Roland 'Bee' Beamont, who would fly Hurricanes in France in 1940 with 87 Squadron recalled, 'a feeling of exhilaration with all this power and being able to get up to 300 miles an hour on the air-speed indicator very easily in a shallow dive at any point in your flight. This was a great experience for an eighteen-year-old'.

When the Hurricane was officially rolled out to the press in 1938 the air correspondent of the *Times* reported, 'The fastest 'plane in service in any air force

BELOW *Work in progress*: Hurricane overhaul, Northolt. At other times aircraft were dispersed around the airfield perimeter to minimise damage from enemy intruders.

in the world was yesterday removed from the Air Ministry's semi-secret list ... The Hurricane is outstanding in its class in respect of duration as well as speed.' The ratio of Hurricanes to Spitfires during the Battle of Britain was consistent at two to one.

All Britain thrilled to the Vickers Supermarine Spitfire. No other aircraft has ever been written about in so authoritative and admiring a manner or achieved such glowing testimonials, summarized in the words of W.G.G. Duncan-Smith: 'A joy to fly, a sureness of robust qualities, a challenge to risk all.' A tribute to the visionary expectations of its chief designer, Reginald Joseph Mitchell.

'R.J.' as he was known, was by any measure a designer of real distinction. His reputation derives from his uncompromising and meticulous approach to producing a

OPPOSITE *Some of the 'Few'*: 242 Squadron returning to Martlesham. Sydney Camm's Hawker Hurricane assumed great importance in the defence of Britain.

BELOW *Battle station*: 'A' Flight, 32 Squadron and ground personnel, Hawkinge. A majority of Fighter Command squadrons were composed of Hurricanes in the summer of 1940.

It is vital to the safety of the nation, that Britain should become a nation of aviators. In matters of defence, we live on an island no longer. The day that Blériot flew the Channel marked the end of an insular safety, and the beginning of the time when Britain must seek another form of defence beside its ships.

SIR ALAN COBHAM

technically advanced monoplane fighter before his untimely death from cancer in 1937, at the age of forty-two. Mitchell, drawing on the racing lineage of his designs for Schneider Trophy winning seaplanes, used a light alloy monocoque fuselage of similar configuration. His objective was a balance of lightness and strength, supreme manouevrability and finesse. And, above all, high performance: Mitchell's Spitfire, capable of 362 mph at 20,000 feet, climbed faster than the Hurricane.

The revolutionary design was distinguishable by his finest achievement in the shape of an elliptical wing to reduce air resistance and increase speed. Beverly Shenstone was Mitchell's aerodynamicist:

RIGHT *Team effort*: 'Mutt' Summers, Vickers chief test pilot (far left), R.J.Mitchell (seated) and Jeffrey Quill (far right).

The elliptical wing was decided upon quite early on. Aerodynamically it was the best for our purpose because the induced drag, that caused lift, was lowest when this shape was used: the ellipse was an ideal shape, theoretically a perfection. There were other advantages as far as we were concerned. To reduce drag we wanted the lowest possible wing thickness-to-chord ratio, consistent with the necessary strength. But near the root the wing had to be thick enough to accommodate the retracted undercarriage and the guns... A straight-tapered wing starts to reduce in chord from the moment it leaves the root; an elliptical wing, on the other hand, tapers only very slowly at first then progressively more rapidly towards the tip.

BELOW *Famous name*: Spitfire in a fighter pen at Tangmere. The unmistakable elliptical wings reduced drag and increased airspeed.

ABOVE *Touching the heights*: advertisement for Vickers Supermarine, makers of the Spitfire. R.J.Mitchell's design achieved an iconic status during the battle which has never faded.

OPPOSITE *Scramble!*: Spitfires of 65 Squadron are scrambled. Frank Usmar recalled, 'When you were running to your machine, the adrenalin took over... Once you got in your aircraft and were roaring away you seemed to have another feeling altogether.'

The prototype of Mitchell's Merlin-engined Spitfire (K5054) was flown on her maiden flight by J. 'Mutt' Summers, chief test pilot of Vickers Aviation, on 5 March 1936. Summers' entry under 'Flying' in his report memorably reads: 'The handling qualities of this machine are remarkably good.' Test pilot Jeffrey Quill, who also flew the prototype, wrote of 'the immediate impression of speed'. Yet Quill, who flew with 65 Squadron during the Battle, remembered:

A lot of people felt that the Spitfire, although it had a very good performance...had been bought at too high a price. In terms of ease of production it was going to be a much more expensive and difficult aeroplane to mass produce. In terms of the ease of maintenance it was going to be a much more complicated aeroplane to look after and service...For instance, you could lower the undercarriage of a Hurricane and take the wings off because the undercarriage was in the centre section...You could take the wings off, put the tail up on a three-ton lorry and tow it along the road. You couldn't do that with a Spitfire. If you took the wings off...it took the undercarriage off as well... There were a lot of people who were against the Spitfire for those practical considerations. Therefore if we had not been able to show a really definite advantage over the Hurricane, it probably wouldn't have been ordered. We were well aware of that.

Vickers Supermarine, following five hundred hours of testing, needed two years to tool up for Spitfire production. New and complex assembly techniques had to be learned to manufacture the all-metal stressed skin, and the fighter took two and a half times longer to build than the Hurricane. Equally, repair and maintenance made time-consuming demands on ground crew.

The first operational Mark I Spitfire was reserved for the crack 19 Squadron at Duxford, and delivered in August 1938 by Jeffrey Quill, who like other leading test pilots, had served with Duxford's Station Flight. By the end of the year both 19 and 66 were re-equipped. Both squadrons were used for intensive flight trials at Duxford, the RAF's first Spitfire station.

Geoffrey Wellum, who served with 92 Squadron throughout the Battle of Britain recounted his experiences with the aircraft in his compelling memoir *First Light*:

Dispersal pen and my Spitfire. I pause and look at her. A long shapely nose, not exactly arrogant but, nevertheless, daring anyone to take a swing at it. Lines beautifully proportioned, the aircraft sitting there, engine turning easily and smoothly with subdued power, the slipstream blows the moisture over the top of the wings in thin streamlets. Flashes of blue flame from the exhausts are easily seen in the half light, an occasional backfire and the whole aeroplane trembling like a thoroughbred at the start of the Derby.

And here is Wellum on approach:

Speed down to under 180 mph. OK, wheels down, select and wait. A reassuring clonk, clonk, and green down light on the panel, pitch fully fine and turn crosswind. Now turn in for the final approach, flaps down, a braking effect just like a dozen men sitting on your wings, trim her out, speed 90 mph, that's nice. I look ahead over the long nose, open and slide back the hood, just a trickle of engine. The hedge of the airfield passes under my wings and the ground comes rapidly closer. Check her. The rate of descent slows, speed dropping away, second check, ease the stick back a bit, a little lower, concentration needed, throttle closed, stick back, don't let the nose drop, stick back still, a wee bit more. The speed drops off, near the point of stall and everything has gone quiet. The nose points upwards and the airscrew idles over in front of me, I can almost count the blades as they pass.

'In 1940' said Roland Beamont, 'the Spitfire was, and still is today, probably the most elegant and beautiful single-seater fighter aeroplane that has ever been built.' Jeffrey Quill, who greatly respected 'the courage and achievement' of Hurricane pilots has the last word:

Generally speaking, ex-Battle of Britain pilots often become a bit partisan on the relative merits of the Hurricane and the Spitfire. The Spitfire achieved, in the eyes of the public, a distinct aura of romance because of its great beauty of line and the ease of recognition in the air, and partly on account of its Schneider ancestry. After many years of reflection I take the view that it took both of them to win the Battle of Britain and neither would have achieved it on their own. The Hurricane achieved the greater damage to the enemy (as has often been pointed out), but without the Spitfire squadrons to fight the 109s their casualties might well have led to the losing of the battle.

Flying is hypnotic and all pilots are willing victims to the spell. Their world is like a magic island in which the factors of life and death assume their proper values. Thinking becomes clear because there are no earthly foibles or embellishments to confuse it. Professional pilots are, of necessity, uncomplicated, simple men. Their thinking must remain straightforward, or they die – violently.

E.K.GANN

LEFT *Squadron Leader*: Alexander Johnstone, 602 Squadron, on approach in his Spitfire, Westhampnett on the Goodwood estate. 'Most pilots used to want to fly the best' said Jeffrey Quill. 'It certainly was the best.'

WAR STORIES

The 'Munich Crisis', a symbol of political misjudgement that keyed up the nation unwillingly for war, attracted enormous publicity in September 1938. 'Crisis off till a Week To-morrow' reported the *Sunday Express*, 'No Sensations Expected.' It was a time of negotiation and compromise over Hitler's occupation of Czechoslovakia, a nation denounced by Luftwaffe chief Hermann Goering as a 'vile race of dwarfs without any culture'. Sir Stafford Cripps on the Opposition benches had accurately forecast that 'Germany's next act of aggression will be directed against Czechoslovakia, and then the people of Great Britain will find themselves back in the days of 1914.' But no one was listening to Stafford Cripps.

At first, the Munich Conference with Hitler appeared successful. Peace was seemingly preserved (British military intelligence had warned of reprisals by the Luftwaffe in the form of strikes on London if war was declared). 'I have no doubt' said Britain's prime minister Neville Chamberlain, who shared this view, 'that my visit alone prevented an invasion for which everything was prepared.'

Across the channel, the French Aviation Minister was certain that 'the destruction of Paris would pass all imagination' and it was believed that the Lutwaffe would flatten French cities in a fortnight. 'We are going blindfold towards an abyss' said the far-sighted French politician Paul Reynaud in a broadcast to his countrymen in November 1938. Of special interest was the assessment of the intelligence section of the Luftwaffe General Staff that the most Nazi-dominated of the three services had exerted decisive political pressure over Munich.

Chamberlain's maiden flight, in a De Havilland Flamingo, for his historic rendezvous with the Führer at Berchtesgaden was tracked from Heston airport by coastal radar. Yet Dowding's essential structure of communications and control rooms, radar stations, Anti-Aircraft Command and Observer Corps posts was still below the safety margin.

OPPOSITE *Waiting for the call*: final peacetime exercise, August 1939. Pilots at rest outside No.5 hangar, Northolt. Sector Stations were the key to the defence of London.

ABOVE *State visit*: exiled leader Eduard Benes visits Czech pilots flying with 310 Squadron. 'I'll give you my word of honour' Goering told the Czech envoy in Berlin, 'Czechoslovakia has nothing to fear from the Reich.'

OPPOSITE *'Matilda'*: a barrage balloon operated by WAAFs, anchored to the ground to deter low-strafing intruders. The contribution of women on the home front, undertaking a variety of roles, was considerable. 'The last war was a soldier's war' reported *Mother and Home* magazine. 'This one is everybody's.'

Since the Czech crisis, thousands had volunteered as air-raid wardens or auxiliaries in the fire-fighting and ambulance services and over a million 'Anderson' shelters were distributed to supposed danger areas. Many people, however, had no gardens in which shelters could be sunk. Trenches had been dug, mothers of babies issued with gas masks and barrage balloons inflated. Yet press reports almost entirely overlooked the question of whether the fighting forces were equipped with the essential striking power to wage modern warfare.

In Berlin Hitler ordered Hermann Goering to construct a 'gigantic armaments programme which would make insignificant all previous achievements'. Goering's Luftwaffe would increase in number five-fold 'to burst upon the foe' quoting Goering, 'like a chorus of revenge.' In London in March 1939 Poland received a Franco-British guarantee to resist German attack.

Also from London, the BBC started broadcasting foreign language news bulletins to counter propaganda from the nationalist anti-parliamentarian rulers in Germany. The *Spectator* expressed the view that 'A week whose first four days have been marked by no accentuation of crisis is by common consent being described as a period of "lull" in international affairs.' Chamberlain, in a letter to his sister in July, wrote: 'Hitler has concluded that we mean business and that the time is not ripe for the major war...' He deluded himself.

The startling news at the end of August that Germany and Russia had signed a 'Non-Aggression' pact resigned the public to the real dangers of the military situation. No more passenger bookings were accepted by Imperial Airways on their Empire routes and ex-RAF pilots who formed the core of the flying staff were recalled to the colours. A number had seen Germany at first hand and knew what the Nazis were like and how they operated. The exchange of diplomatic notes continued but the Long Weekend was nearly over.

Adolf Hitler was the only man in Europe who was willing to move his troops across a hostile frontier defended by specific guarantees and therefore risk a European war. No one else was. On 3 September his refusal to withdraw forces from Poland led to Chamberlain's radio broadcast to the nation declaring that 'this country is at war with

In the afternoon of 2 September the ten Battle Squadrons of the Advanced Air Striking Force winged their way across to the heart of the champagne country, landed, re-fuelled and bombed up. When, shortly after eleven o'clock the following morning, the embittered accents of a disillusioned Prime Minister announced that we were at war with Germany, the Royal Air Force, if not complete down to the last button on the last Mae West, was ready – and more than willing.

DENIS RICHARDS, *THE FIGHT AT ODDS*

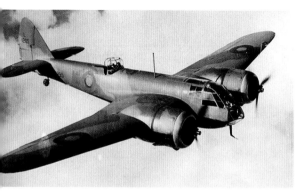

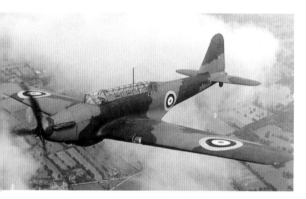

ABOVE *Battle order*: six squadrons of outmoded Bristol Blenheim tactical bombers flew in the battle (top). Pilots flying unescorted daylight raids in the ground support Fairey Battle (below) during the Battle of France found themselves in a death-trap.

Germany.' His speech was followed by the first air-raid warning siren. A false alarm as it turned out. In his memoir *Time and Chance* Peter Townsend, whose squadron was based at Tangmere, headed for the Old Ship at Bosham: 'What a party we had: at closing time, we went out into the street and fired our revolvers into the air. Windows were flung open, people rushed from their houses, thinking the invasion had started.'

In the first week of war Dowding's overwhelming concern was Fighter Command's defensive strength. He estimated that 52 squadrons were needed for the defence of Britain but of 39 squadrons under his command, four went to France, flying reconnaissance missions and protecting the British Expeditionary Force against Luftwaffe attacks, and another four were deployed to protect convoys and naval bases. The Air Council, in response to Dowding's plea for a further twelve fighter squadrons, agreed to the formation of only two units. The swift collapse of the Polish Air Force under the striking power of the Luftwaffe gave Dowding the excellent reason to renew his request in a letter to the Air Staff on 25 September:

> The home defence organisation must not be regarded as co-equal with other commands, but it should receive priority over all other claims until it is firmly secured, since the continued existence of the nation and all its services depends upon the Royal Navy and Fighter Command.

In October the Air Council agreed that Fighter Command should be increased to 60 squadrons within a year but monthly production of single-engined fighters was slow. None of the new squadrons was equipped with modern aircraft.

Hitler's ideological vision of bringing about a total demographic and racial reordering of the globe was advanced by his invasion of France and the Low Countries on 10 May 1940. The offensive marked the end of a strange unreal interlude called the 'Phoney War', a phrase commonly attributed to American journalists. On the same day Chamberlain, obliged to take Winston Churchill into the cabinet at the outbreak of war – as First Sea Lord – was succeeded by him as Prime Minister. Churchill was, in the words of one *Times* journalist 'so much *the* war-leader'.

The small scale British Expeditionary Force sent to the front line in France was supported by the Advanced Air Striking Force, based at Rheims. Odds favoured the enemy. The AASF's Hurricane and outclassed Battle and Blenheim aircraft operated without the advantage of prepared bases and Fighter Command's warning and direction system, which could only work on the home front. RAF pilots faced the challenge of a highly trained Luftwaffe, experienced in fast-moving mobile operations from improvised airfields.

Dowding's operational strength stood at 53 squadrons, six of them on the Continent. In the first three days of the land battle he was required to send the equivalent of six

Successive Secretaries of State for Air and the Air Staff were proved correct in their forecast that there would be no international agreement. Unfortunately at about that time it also became apparent that Britain had already fallen behind Germany in the race for air force expansion, that there was little or no hope of catching up before war broke out and that a long period would still be needed, after the beginning of hostilities, for Britain to get her war production machine into top gear... the war in the air must begin with a strategy of 'close defence' to protect, above all, London and the south-east from a knock out blow...

N.H.GIBBS, *GRAND STRATEGY*

LEFT *Second line of defence*: the two squadrons of Boulton-Paul Defiants lacked forward armament and manoeuvrability, and were no match for German fighters. Defiants, withdrawn from daylight operations after unsustainable loss rates, served in a night-fighter role during the Blitz.

ABOVE *A Passion for Wings*: Churchill took flying lessons but Clementine, his wife, disapproved, urging him to fly 'only with the very best pilot.' Churchill assured her flying was 'not at all dangerous' but on the brink of taking his pilot's certificate gave up, to Clemmie's express relief.

additional squadrons to France and two to Norway, making, as he wrote, 'very serious calls' upon the Home Defence Fighter units. On 14 May the War Cabinet agreed to French Premier Paul Reynaud's call for ten more squadrons. Dowding, who later wrote that 'I saw my resources slipping away like sand in an hourglass' appeared before the Cabinet at his own request on the following day.

Dowding appealed against the detachment of even more fighters, handing Churchill a one-page graph in red ink (mistaken by some present for his resignation) showing that the current loss rate of Hurricanes in France was unsustainable and would lead to nil reserves. The Head of Fighter Command returned home 'in a mood of desperation'. To his 'inexpressible relief', however, it was agreed that no more fighters should be sent to France in the short term and that Bomber Command assaults on the Ruhr should be made in an attempt to divert the Luftwaffe from the battle for France.

Elsewhere events were piling up: the lightning pace of the German advance threatened the whole Allied position in the north. It was agreed that four more squadrons would be despatched across the Channel. Following a flying visit to Paris on 16 May Churchill, 'to give the last chance to the French army to rally its bravery and strength', asked the Cabinet to approve sending another six units. On the same day Dowding drafted a vivid appreciation of the situation:

> I would remind the Air Council that the last estimate which they made as to the force necessary to defend this country was 52 squadrons, and my strength has now been reduced to the equivalent of 36 squadrons.
>
> Once a decision has been reached as to the limit on which the Air Council and the Cabinet are prepared to stake the existence of the country, it should be made clear to the Allied Commanders on the Continent that not a single aeroplane from Fighter Command beyond the limit will be sent across the Channel, no matter how desperate the situation may become.
>
> I must point out that within the last few days the equivalent of 10 squadrons have been sent to France, that the Hurricane Squadrons remaining in this country are seriously depleted, and that the more squadrons which are sent to France the higher will be the wastage and the more insistent the demands for reinforcements.

Dowding's conclusion did credit to British self assurance as to the eventual outcome of the battle:

> If an adequate fighter force is kept in this country, if the fleet remains in being, and if Home Forces are suitably organized to resist invasion, we should be able to carry on the war single handed for some time, if not indefinitely. But, if the Home Defence Force is drained away in desperate attempts to remedy the situation in France, defeat in France will involve the final, complete and irremediable defeat of this country.

On the same day Sir Cyril Newall, Chief of the Air Staff, agreed to commit six more Hurricane squadrons to France. The plan for squadrons to operate from battered and exposed French airfields was frustrated by the worsening situation and it was agreed that three squadrons of reinforcements should be flown over to forward airfields in the morning, relieved by the other three in the afternoon. 'I do not believe' wrote Newall the next day, 'that to throw in a few more fighter squadrons, whose loss might vitally weaken the fighter line at home, would make the difference between victory and defeat in France.' By 19 May the situation was rendered hopeless and that day Churchill ordered:

> No more squadrons of fighters will leave for France. If it becomes necessary to evacuate the B.E.F. a very strong covering operation will be necessary from English bases against German bombers who will certainly do their best to prevent embarkation.

A week later Operation Dynamo – the evacuation of the cornered B.E.F. driven back to the coast at Dunkirk by the *blitzkrieg* – saw the Admiralty muster every seaworthy vessel it could to rescue the besieged forces from the beaches. Fighter Command's depleted squadrons, covering the troop withdrawal from English airfields, were compromised by flying at the limit of their range, with minimal time over the harbour area. The first decisive encounters between Spitfires and the Luftwaffe took place above the Dunkirk perimeter, in an attempt to break up constant Ju 87 Stuka dive bomber

My parachute caught in a tree so I undid my harness and slid down the trunk. There was a battle going on nearby; I could not see anything but there was an exchange of small-arms fire not very far away. What was incongruous was that the birds were making nearly as much noise as the guns: it was about 6 o'clock in the morning and this was the dawn chorus. I had come down near Villiers, which seemed appropriate as it happened to be my middle name.

MILES DELAP, 82 SQUADRON

ABOVE *Me 109*: Robin Wight, 213 Squadron, wrote during Dunkirk, 'Well, another day is gone, and with it a lot of grand blokes. Got another brace of 109s today, but the whole Luftwaffe seems to leap on us – we were hopelessly outnumbered'.

'Crew after crew', declared Antoine St.Exupéry, iconic French author and aviator, 'was being offered up as a sacrifice. It was as if you dashed glassfuls of water into a forest fire in the hope of putting it out.'

attacks. Brian Kingcome in *A Willingness to Die* described from the air the flash and thud of shell-fire on the beaches:

> ...littered with the smoking wreckage of engines and equipment...The sands erupted into huge geysers from exploding bombs and shells, while a backdrop to the scene of carnage and destruction was provided by the palls of oily black smoke rising from the burning harbour and houses...and hanging high in the still air. And yet there the orderly line of our troops stood, chaos and Armageddon at their backs, patiently waiting their turn to wade into the sea.

The 'miracle of Dunkirk' was the safe return of over 338,000 British and Allied troops. The *Daily Mirror* headline said it all: 'Bloody Marvellous.' Fighter Command pilots, in the air two, three or sometimes even four times a day between England and northern France and conscious of their own exhaustion and losses, took stock: between 10 May and 20 June, 284 pilots were killed and 477 fighters lost. At the time of the French surrender on 17 June all Hurricane and Spitfire squadrons were below strength and only two thirds of them were ready for operations.

On the following day Churchill uttered a memorable warning to the House of Commons:

> What General Weygand called the Battle of France is over. I expect that the Battle of Britain is about to begin. Upon the battle depends the survival of Christian civilisation. Upon it depends our own British life and the long continuity of our institutions and our Empire. The whole fury and might of the enemy must very soon be turned on us. Hitler knows that he will have to break us in this island or lose the war. If we can stand up to him, all Europe will be free, and the life of the world may move forward into broad, sunlit uplands, but if we fail, then the

whole world, including the United States, and all that we have known and cared for, will sink into the abyss of a new dark age made more sinister, and perhaps more protracted, by the lights of a perverted science.

Let us therefore brace ourselves to our duty and so bear ourselves that if the British Empire and its Commonwealth lasts for a thousand years men will still say, 'This was their finest hour.'

The real test for Fighter Command was yet to come.

BELOW *In flight*: Peter Vacher's restored Hawker Hurricane Mark I, a Battle of Britain veteran and rare survivor of 14,500 Hurricanes built.

THE RISE AND RISE OF THE LUFTWAFFE

It is a measure of the original high estimates formed by the German air force that General Quade, former commandant of the Luftwaffe Staff College, was able to record in July 1940:

> The situation as it presents itself for our Air Force for the decisive struggle against Britain is as favourable as it can be...What will happen when the German Air Force employs its whole strength against England? The game looks bad for England and her geographical and military isolation. We can face with confidence the great decision to come!

I tell you, if the Führer wishes it, then two times two is five.

REICHSMARSCHAL
HERMANN GOERING

Germany's air fleet was dissolved in 1919 and manufacture of military aircraft forbidden under the terms of the Treaty of Versailles. In response, General Hans von Seeckt, employed by the Defence Ministry, set up a secret military flying school at Lipetsk, south-east of Moscow. The ministry in Berlin included a number of high-ranking figures who would play leading roles in the Battle of Britain: Sperrle, Stumpff, Kesselring and Wolfram von Richtofen, one of the pioneers of formation flying, among them.

Sports aviation, permissible in Germany and Austria under the Versailles Treaty, was encouraged to train new pilots and by 1929 membership of state-sponsored light aeroplane and glider clubs – the *Luftsportsverband* – exceeded 50,000. In 1926, the lifting of restrictions on the size and number of Germany's civil aircraft led to the formation of the monopolistic Lufthansa airline. The company's first chairman was Erhard Milch, a hugely capable organiser who was responsible for air travel during the 'Hitler over Germany' election campaign and chief architect of the Lutwaffe. Standards of training for the pilots of the new airline were rigorous: of 4,000 candidates entered for

OPPOSITE *Menace from the air*: Messerschmitt Me 110s firmly on the offensive. By 1939, the Luftwaffe could muster over 3,750 aircraft of all types, all manned by well-trained aircrews.

Lufthansa's Air Transport course in 1932, only 18 were accepted – future Battle of Britain fighter ace Adolf Galland was one of them.

The Luftwaffe, the most formidable air fleet in the world, was officially announced by Hitler on 1 March 1935. Hermann Goering, the former World War One fighter pilot who succeeded Baron Manfred von Richtofen in command of the 'flying circus' in 1917, took overall charge. One of the big guns among the Nazi gangsters, with a taste for swaggering about in bizarre military costume, 'the fat man' was the Führer's most powerful lieutenant. A cunning, ruthless and corrupt party member, his favoured standing with Hitler gave him substantial independence (to the cost of his aircrews). Goering, who declined to read documents longer than four pages and had no head for statistics, once remarked that 'The Führer does not ask me how big my bombers are but how many there are.'

A major influence on the rise and rise of the Luftwaffe was the outbreak of the Spanish Civil War in 1936. Germany's *Legion Kondor*, whose emblem was fittingly a swooping condor clasping a bomb in its talons, was commanded by Hugo Sperrle. Wolfram von Richtofen, his Chief of Staff, perceived the conflict as a testing ground for tactics by the first generation of Luftwaffe pilots such as Galland and Werner Moelders, A contest, in von Richtofen's view, that was 'a trial in totalitarian warfare'.

The vulnerability of a civilian population to assault by massed formations from the air was demonstrated by the attack on a defenceless Guernica, inspiring Picasso's enduring masterpiece. A bombing raid where Condor Legion pilots strafed the town's inhabitants at 200 feet, and a priest extinguished an incendiary bomb with communion wine. One eyewitness said it resembled 'having a preview of the end of the world'. In America *The New York Times* reported, 'This climax of cruelty horrifies the world more than any other barbarity of a barbarous war.' In a confidential signal to Berlin, von Richtofen claimed the 'concentrated attack' as 'the greatest success.' Aerial *Blitzkrieg* – later refined by von Richtofen in Poland – played a decisive role in Franco's victory in Spain.

In 1940, the pilots of Fighter Command steeled themselves to challenge a Luftwaffe disposed for operations against Britain in three air fleets (*Luftflotten*) answering directly to Goering and Milch. The newly formed Air Fleet 5, based in Scandinavia, under

General Hans-Juergen Stumpff, and the two main Air Fleets 2 and 3, with headquarters in Brussels and Paris, led respectively by Albert Kesselring, a successful career soldier who became Chief of the Luftwaffe General Staff in 1936, and Condor Legion veteran Hugo Sperrle. Both were middle-aged Bavarians, both promoted by Hitler to the rank of Field Marshal in July 1940, and both commanders of considerable professional ability.

The primary purpose of the enemy's air campaign in the summer of 1940 was to reduce the RAF's capacity to fight and to establish and maintain full mastery of the air. A mixed force of fighters and light and medium bombers was sent over the Channel to drive Fighter Command from the sky. Luftwaffe plans for a long-range heavy bomber had been discontinued in favour of the lighter, faster single- and twin-engined aircraft carrying a restricted bomb-load.

The Junkers Ju 87B, or Stuka, was a two-seat dive bomber inspired by the American

> We dived into them [Stukas] and they went down to 100 feet above the water. Then followed a running chase out to sea. The evasive action they took was to throttle back and do steep turns to right and left, so that we would overshoot. There were, however, so many of them that if one was shaken off the tail of one there was always another one to sit on.
>
> ERIC MARRS, 152 SQUADRON

OPPOSITE *Field Marshals*: (top) Erhard Milch, prime architect of the Luftwaffe. (Below) Hugo Sperrle, whose personal headquarters of Air Fleet 3 were situated in fashionable Deauville. Sperrle pressed for concentrated attacks to be continued on Fighter Command airfields. He was, fortunately, overruled.

LEFT *Stuka*: a steep dive attack by a Ju 87 was supremely effective in striking a defended target.

ABOVE LEFT *Spoils of war*: cutting a section of tailplane from a downed aircraft for display as a squadron trophy was a popular sport.

ABOVE RIGHT *Ju 88*: Hugo Junkers' 'Wonder Bomber' was the Luftwaffe's newest dive-bomber. The Ju 88 carried a limited bomb load and was never fast enough to outrun defending fighters in daylight.

Curtiss Hawk. A low wing cantilever monoplane with a fixed undercarriage, distinguishable by cranked wings and equipped with dive-brakes to control air speed in a near-vertical dive. A siren was fitted to terrorise victims in its line of flight. Slow and unmanoeuvrable, the Stuka was no match for the Hurricane and Spitfire. Goering ordered that 'Until the enemy fighter force has been broken, Stuka units are only to be used when circumstances are particularly favourable.' After heavy losses Ju 87s were withdrawn from the Battle of Britain.

The Ju 88A, the Luftwaffe's newest and most effective medium bomber, was a twin-engined monoplane capable of high speeds and, in the words of Wing Commander Ken MacKenzie, 'a notoriously strong aircraft and difficult to shoot down.' Its defensive armament was weak, similar to that of the low-wing, twin-engined Heinkel 111, an earlier bomber design judged to be obsolete in many ways and too slow in combat during the battle. The high-wing Dornier Do 17 bomber, originally designed as a fast mail plane for Lufthansa and known as the 'Flying Pencil', was equally obsolescent by 1940. Both the He 111 and Do 17 were vulnerable to fighter attack.

In the Battle of Britain the Luftwaffe's bomber force was screened by two types of escort fighter built at the *Bayerische Flugzeugwerke* and originally prefixed Bf. The Messerschmitt Bf 110 was a long-range, all metal low-wing cantilever monoplane, fitted with twin fins and rudders and powered by two engines. Pilot and gunner-navigator shared a long plexiglass enclosed cockpit and during the battle the Me 110,

LEFT *Air Power*: Heinkel IIIs in 'stepped' formation. 'Ural', Germany's plan for a long-range heavy bomber, was dropped in 1936. Thereafter, the Luftwaffe's power to damage targets of strategic importance was limited.

BELOW *The 'Flying Pencil'*: Claude Dornier's medium bomber was popular with aircrew. The long-serving Do 17 flew extensively in the battle, suffering heavily from fighter attack.

RIGHT *Me 110s*: declared Goering, would
be assembled in 'destroyer (*zerstörer*)
units' and would form 'the strategic elite
of the Luftwaffe.' Not all shared his
optimism and his prediction, one of
many, was never destined to be fulfilled.

OPPOSITE *A Foreign Field*: the Me 110
was deployed to provoke a decisive
engagement with defending fighters.
During the battle over France, dinner at
Maxim's was promised to the first pilot
to claim a Me 110.

equipped with formidable nose armament, was deployed to draw enemy fighters into the air. Fighter Command saw through this manoeuvre very early.

The Messerschmitt's Bf 109E was the star turn in the newly blooded German air force. Willy Emil Messerschmitt, like Sydney Camm and Reginald Mitchell, was one of the foremost aircraft designers of the age, responsible for wide-ranging designs that included a succession of record-breaking gliders and the jet-powered Me 262. In 1934, in answer to a German Air Ministry specification for a new fighter with retractable undercarriage and a top speed of 280 mph, Messerschmitt designed a lightweight, low-drag monoplane capable of housing the most powerful engine under development.

The trials prototype, curiously enough powered by an imported Rolls-Royce Kestrel engine, was first flown by Hans 'Bubi' Knoetzsch in May 1935. Messerchmitt's innovative design was admired by another experienced pilot, Johannes Trautloft, who tested early Me 109s sent out to Spain in 1937. Trautloft recorded that 'The new Bf 109 looks fabulous. The take-off certainly is unusual, but as soon as I am in the air I feel at home in the new bird. Its flight characteristics are fantastic... To fly the Bf 109 is really a joy.' Luftwaffe pilot Heinz Knoke found the new fighter 'difficult to handle and dangerous at first'.

A low-wing, all metal cantilever monoplane, the fuselage covered with a flush-riveted duralumin skin, the Me 109 was armed with cannon and heavy calibre machine-guns.

RIGHT *High performer*: Willy Messerschmitt's masterpiece, the most feared aircraft in the Luftwaffe line-up. The 357mph Me 109, powered by a Daimler-Benz supercharged engine, was superior to the opposition above 20,000 feet. Highly effective in 'free-chase', 109s were less convincing when escorting bombers (insisted on by Goering). Lack of range was a decisive factor but 20mm cannon provided real striking power.

OPPOSITE LEFT *Loading up*: nose armament for the Me 110 fighter. The Luftwaffe was short of combat-ready fighters during the first stage of the battle due to operational shortcomings. Most German aircraft types in the battle were still in service years later.

OPPOSITE RIGHT *Pilot's briefing*: the Luftwaffe's reputation was at its height at the start of the battle, Werner Kriepe, Air Fleet 3 chief of operations, stated '…the pilots were highly skilled…Their moral was very high and they were confident of victory.

Cockpit space was confined and visibility limited but pilots were protected by back and front armour during the battle. The narrow-track undercarriage fixed to the fuselage and folding outwards resulted in countless accidents on landing. Over five per cent of all Me 109 losses were attributed to this cause. A three-blade automatic variable pitch propeller offered superior handling but performance was compromised by short endurance – marginally over one hour's flying time at full throttle.

Aerodynamically efficient, highly manoeuvrable and with a very fast rate of climb, the production Me 109 was powered by a Daimler-Benz supercharged engine that prevented stalling in a steep dive. Top speed was 357 mph and above 20,000 feet Me 109s were reckoned to be unrivalled. The service ceiling was an impressive 36,000 feet. The first Me 109s, type E-I and know to Luftwaffe pilots as the 'Emil', were delivered in 1939. By the end of the war over 33,000 had been built – a record figure for combat aircraft in the Second World War.

HONOUR IN DEFENCE

*Churchill, the saviour
of his country*

A.J.P. TAYLOR,
OXFORD HISTORY OF ENGLAND

OPPOSITE *'Finger four' formation*:
Me 109s over the Channel. A total of
2,800 aircraft were set the task by
Goering, confident of an aerial
masterstroke, of gaining air supremacy.
Luftwaffe pilots had the edge in combat
during the first phase of the battle.

Hitler, master of Europe, looked across the Channel from Cap Gris Nez Calais in June 1940 and contemplated his next step in the west. He became interested in a pact with London. A memorandum by General Jodl prepared in the same month expressed the Führer's view that Britain 'should be inclined to make peace when she learns she can still get it now at relatively little cost'.

Goering, no adherent of invasion, sought to conduct an independent air offensive against Britain 'owing to the inadequate air defences of the island' and proposed strikes against her ports and cities. His Führer, however, hankered after expansion of the German empire to the east. 'Now that Britain will presumably be willing to make peace' he told one of his service leaders on 2 June, 'I will begin the final settlement of scores with Bolshevism.'

Hitler's preference was a political and diplomatic settlement. He was conscious of the limits of enforcing surrender by blockade and was particularly sensitive to the hazards of crossing a frequently rough, tidal channel. Colonel-General Franz Halder stated that 'Invasion is to be undertaken only if no other way is left to bring terms to Britain.'

The prospect of invasion was first raised with Hitler by Grand Admiral Erich Raeder in May and June 1940. Raeder observed that no invasion fleet could cross the English Channel while Fighter Command stood undefeated in their path. Both the Naval staff and Army chiefs distrusted Goering, questioning his Luftwaffe's ability to attain air superiority.

Meanwhile, Luftwaffe units recovering from heavy losses in France and Norway and expected to provide aerial artillery in direct support of a full-scale invasion, were established on aerodromes in France, the Low Countries and Norway. On 25 June, one of Hitler's secretaries recorded: 'The Chief plans to speak to the Reichstag shortly. It will probably be his last appeal to Britain. If they don't come round even then, he will proceed without pity...'

Winston Churchill demonstrated no inclination to learn of peace terms from Berlin. At the time of the Dunkirk evacuation his military advisers informed him that Germany 'has most of the cards; but the real test is whether the morale of our fighting personnel and civil population will counter-balance the numerical and material advantages which Germany enjoys. We believe it will'. The American war correspondent Virginia Cowles was struck by the spirit of the nation: 'For the first time I understood what the maxim meant: "England never knows when she is beaten"... I was more than flabbergasted. I not only understood the maxim; I understood why Britain never had been beaten.'

BELOW *'Sea Lion'*: barges and transports at Germany's disposal. Attacks on the invasion ports were a sharp reminder of the offensive strength of Bomber and Fighter Command.

On 16 July, in the absence of news from his intermediaries. Hitler issued War Directive No.16 for a landing on the southern English coastline. The operation was code-named 'Sea Lion.' He ordered preparations to be ready by the middle of August and sea routes to be secured, declaring that 'The English Air Force must be eliminated to such an extent that it will be incapable of putting up any substantial opposition to the invading troops.' Speaking from the Kroll Opera House in Berlin three days later, he made 'a final appeal to reason and common sense.' Count Gallenzo Ciano was witness to the Riechstag speech, '...when the first cold British reactions to the speech arrive, a sense of ill-concealed disappointment spreads among the Germans.' The Italian Foreign Minister was convinced Hitler 'would like an understanding with Great Britain. He knew that war with the British will be hard and bloody'. Copies of the speech, dropped over England at high altitude, were briskly auctioned on behalf of the Red Cross.

Hitler was under no illusion about the task of overcoming a 'defensively prepared and utterly determined enemy.' He told his commanders at a naval conference on 21 July that 'complete mastery of the air' was vital, insisting that Channel weather conditions demanded that 'the main operation must be completed by 15 September'. Air co-operation was decisive and, he stressed, 'must be regarded as the principal factor in fixing the date... If it not certain that preparations can be completed by the beginning of September, other plans must be considered'.

Naval, military and aerial forces were assembled for invasion, but conflicting views and doubts among the German High Command were encapsulated by one senior figure, Walter Warlimont, who wrote of 'the morass of uncertainty in which German strategy was labouring during this period'. The German Naval Staff reported that 'The task allotted to the Navy is out of all proportion to its strength. It cannot be assumed that the Luftwaffe alone will succeed in keeping the enemy naval forces clear of our shipping, as its operations are very dependent upon weather conditions.'

ABOVE *Kanalkampf*: Goering (first right) and his staff look towards the chalk cliffs of Dover, 1940. Churchill wrote, 'whatever our shortcomings, we understand sea affairs very thoroughly.' 'The German soldier' remarked one German Admiral, 'is sick if he crosses the Rhine.'

On 30 June, Goering ordered that 'As long as the enemy air force is not defeated, the prime requirement is to attack it, by day and by night, in the air.' General Hans Jeschonnek, his Chief of General Staff, was disposed to conclude: 'The Führer has no intention of mounting an invasion... There won't be any invasion, and I have no time to waste on planning one.' Whatever the truth of that, Hitler had given 'Operation Sea Lion' highest priority and, to observers across the Channel, preparations appeared too far advanced for a mere bluff. The spectre of invasion remained.

Dowding's system to command and control his squadrons in action to counter the threat of invasion and aerial bombardment was centred on Command Headquarters at Bentley Priory. By July 1940, Fighter Command was quartered into 10 Group, covering the south-west, 11 Group to the south-east, 12 Group based in central England, and 13 Group extending to the north.

The underground Filter Room at Bentley Priory acted as a telephone exchange for information. Chain Home stations generally detected German raids forming up over the Calais or Cotentin Peninsula area and the plot – once established – was 'told'

As the British fighters are controlled from the ground by radio-telephone their forces are tied to their respective ground stations and are thereby restrained in mobility, even taking into consideration the probability that the ground stations are partly mobile. Consequently, the assembly of strong fighter forces at determined points and at short notice is not to be expected.

LUFTWAFFE REPORT, 7 AUGUST 1940

through to the Filter Room by landline. This information was relayed to the adjacent Operations Room, nerve centre of the system, on a grid map on the 'ops' table.

Enemy formations were plotted by members of the Women's Auxiliary Air Force receiving instructions over headsets. By means of magnetic croupier-style rakes WAAFs postioned numbered marker blocks in yellow, red or blue to represent enemy aircraft. American Military attaché Raymond Lee described the process for readers of the *London Observer*:

> We went down, down, down into great subterranean chambers where in two great rooms, two of the most intricate and modern organisations of the world are housed. In one room is the huge map on which moment by moment the reports

RIGHT *Official War Artist*: Felix Topolski's drawing of the improvised Operations Room set up in a Sussex school room following a heavy raid on Tangmere, 16 August 1940.

ABOVE *Time zones*: a colour-coded clock in every Operations Room allowed Controllers to assess 'plots' as a raid developed.

LEFT *Command and control*: 10 Group Operations Room, Rudloe Manor, Box, Wiltshire. It is hard to overstate the advantage of radar in directing defending squadrons onto enemy formations. In 1940, the RAF possessed the world's best aerial defence system.

of enemy locations are plotted and enemy air and sea movement exposed, in another an even greater chart where actions are followed... The great rooms are almost silent... only a soft murmur of voices as messages come and go over headsets, and only a little movement as operators move counters and markers from point to point and others tend electric bulletins and switchboards... I had no idea the British could evolve and operate so intricate, so scientific and rapid and organistion...

The process took about four minutes, yet the Luftwaffe, quoting Sandy Johnstone, 'set up attack plans almost at will' and in six minutes flew the distance from Calais to Dover. Successful interception depended on accurate and timely information and colours of the markers changed every five minutes according to a colour-coded clock, allowing Controllers to replace a 'stale' plot with a 'fresh' one.

Sightings by the Observer Corps were passed to a local control centre and onto Sector Stations and Groups, before reaching Bentley Priory. Command headquarters also controlled the Air Raid Warning System. 'Warning Districts' were based on the national telephone network: 'Yellow' warnings were issued when a raid was 20 minutes distant, and emergency services alerted; a 'Red' warning followed five minutes later, when sirens were sounded and anti-aircraft batteries started up; a 'Green' signal marked the 'all clear.'

The location of enemy formations was relayed to Group headquarters and the Sector Stations, all with their own 'Ops' rooms. Each Group determined which sectors to order into the air, and Sector airfields were responsible for the decision to scramble pilots. Once airborne, pilots were vectored by R/T – D/F (Radio-Telephony Directional Finding) to the correct altitude ('angels') for interception. Pilots ordered to 'pancake' (return to base to refuel and reload) were at greatest

BELOW *Observer Corps*: at the outbreak of war, 30,000 observers, plotting aircraft visually, manned one thousand posts. Height estimation was a challenge and observers were inclined to report thunderstorms and flocks of birds as raiders overhead.

risk from a third or fourth wave of enemy action and one of the Controllers' chief duties was maintaining a constant watch on the state of his own squadrons.

It was the task of the front-line airfields of No.11 Group to defend London and the south-east in the forthcoming battle. No.11 Group was led by New Zealander, Air Vice-Marshal Keith (later Sir Keith) Park, who had served in the Royal Flying Corps in 1917, and by the time of Munich was Dowding's right-hand man. The partnership of Dowding the strategic planner, and Park the tactical commander, was looked on as an undoubted success, and could hardly have been in greater contrast to Park's relationship with Trafford (later Sir Trafford) Leigh-Mallory, in command of No.12 Group. There was no denying Leigh-Mallory's organisational qualities but the two men were opposites without mutual attraction. Leigh-Mallory's pointed criticism of Park's tactics resulted in the 'Big Wing' controversy during the battle in September and October.

A highly decorated South African airman, Air Vice-Marshal Sir Quintin Brand, who had shot down a Gotha bomber in the final raid of the First World War, was given command of No.10 Group. Air Vice-Marshal Richard Saul was the highly respected commander of No.13 Group, essentially forming a strategic reserve.

So, as Gerrmany sought to gain a verdict by command of the skies, the scene was set for the opening of an air offensive of the greatest consequence. The morale of the hitherto unstoppable Luftwaffe, convinced of their invincibility, was unquestionably high. Yet as the resourceful and experienced crewmen prepared to engage in the *Kanalkampf* there was incessant talk of frequently hostile weather, and the limited prospect of rescue in the unforgiving English Channel. This forecast was impressively close to the mark.

RIGHT *Rivalry*: Keith Park (above) distinguished himself as an outstanding and determined commander, maintaining high morale by regularly visiting pilots in his Hurricane OKI. Park came into conflict over 'Big Wing' formations with Sir Trafford Leigh-Mallory (below), the assertive and ambitious commander of 12 Group. Park argued that early engagement of the raiders was necessary to protect his airfields. 'Johnnie' Johnson, 616 Squadron ace, considered the 'Big Wing' was 'never particularly successful because of the time it took to form up.' Dowding elected not to intervene in the dispute.

CHURCHILL'S 'FEW'

Aircrew of Fighter Command won their spurs in the Battle of Britain. Airmanship in the form of defining the limits had to be learned, not assumed, and leadership in the fighter business needed a special approach, leading by example and personality. There was a unique sort of glamour surrounding Dowding's 'Fighter Boys'. The typical fighter pilot behaved heroically, but played it down – ideally effort was perceived as selfless and collective. Yet we can salute their courage and utterly responsible approach to battle, showing coolness of judgement, concentration and a proper degree of aggression. Every fighter pilot, however tough and resolute, was acquainted with the second enemy: fear.

Flight has always fired the imagination. Lawrence of Arabia regarded conquest of the air as the most important task of his generation. To many others of both sexes, climbing to a great height and remaining aloft for hours was the first recreation of the age. There was a marked enthusiasm for private flying due to improved standards of airworthiness in design and maintenance, the development of the light aeroplane and the founding of amateur flying clubs. Slogans such as 'Be Up to Date and Aviate' caught the public imagination. You could even buy an aeroplane at Selfridges.

Between the wars, in a period of rearmament, campaigns to recruit volunteers for the RAF appeared regularly. 'Here is *your* opportunity' ran one Air Ministry advertisement, 'to satisfy your ambition. You'll be well paid. You'll find every facility for sport. You'll be among the grandest company you could wish for. You, too, will be flying in the world's finest aeroplanes.' 'It was very pleasant to be with a number of young men of one's age' said John Nicholas, who joined 65 Squadron in 1937, 'most of whom believed in the same things.'

Chamberlain's rearmament programme offered thousands of young men the chance to join the best flying club in the world. One source in the constant search for potential pilots was the expanding University air squadron schemes at Oxford, Cambridge and London. Geoffrey Page, a natural pilot, reading engineering at London, found his

> *'They are not buried yet. We have no time to lose.'*
>
> FIELD MARSHAL ERHARD MILCH, 5 JUNE 1940

OPPOSITE *Biggin's best*: 79 Squadron pilots scamble during Air Defence Exercises, 1939. 'The essence of combat flying' said Roland Beamont, 'was to know your aeroplane's absolute limits so that when you were called upon to use them you could actually get to the limits of the performance without endangering you or your aeroplane.'

lifelong enthusiasm for flying inspired by a venerated First World War ace. His expectations were:

BELOW *Between sorties*: 17 Squadron pilots, Dcbdcn, August 1940. David Hanson (far left) was one of 544 airmen lost in the battle. A further 795 Battle of Britain aircrew failed to return during the war.

boyishly clear and simple. All I wanted to be was a fighter pilot like my hero Captain Albert Ball. I knew practically all there was to know about Albert Ball, how he flew, how he fought, how he won his Victoria Cross, how he died. I also thought I knew about war in the air. I imagined it to be Arthurian – about chivalry. . . death and injury had no part in it.

BELOW *Between sorties*: 17 Squadron pilots, Dcbdcn, August 1940. David Hanson (far left) was one of 544 airmen lost in the battle. A further 795 Battle of Britain aircrew failed to return during the war.

Roy's decision to join the RAF is a great sorrow to me. We have had many arguments but to no avail. 'If there is a war', I said, 'you will never know freedom again.' He replied, 'It is a good life and I like the open air, my mind is made up.' I feel broken-hearted and defeated. If only his father supported me but he aids and abets him, as it were.

DIARY OF CONSTANCE MARCHAND, MOTHER OF ROY MARCHAND, 73 SQUADRON

LEFT *Model behaviour*: 253 Squadron recognition lecture by a blast pen, Kenley. Positive identification of hostile aircraft in limited visibility during the heat of battle was a matter of life and death.

My dear Fighter Boys,

I don't send out many congratulatory letters and signals, but I feel that I must take this occasion, when the intensive fighting in Northern France is for the time being over, to tell you how proud I am of you and the way in which you have fought since the 'Blitzrieg' started.

I wish I could have spent my time visiting you and hearing your accounts of the fighting, but I have occupied myself in working for you in other ways.

I want you to know that my thoughts are always with you, and that it is you and your fighting spirit which will crack the morale of the German Air Force and preserve our Country through the trials which yet lie ahead.

Good luck to you,

H.C.T.DOWDING, AIR CHIEF MARSHAL

By 1939, the Oxford University Air Squadron (OUAS) alone accounted for nearly 500 officers in the RAF.

'I'd always wanted to fly,' said Charlton Haw, who applied to join the RAF, aged eighteen, 'from when I was a small boy. I never wanted to do anything else, really, but I just didn't think there would ever be a chance for me. Until the RAFVR was formed, for a normal schoolboy, it was almost impossible.'

The composition of the reserve forces, the weekend fliers of the Auxiliary Air Force, founded in 1925, and the RAFVR, created in 1936, was well expressed by Ken MacKenzie in *Hurricane Combat*:

> The Auxiliary squadrons, with full squadron status and aircraft establishment administration and station facilities and personnel were rather unique. The pilots were mostly men slightly older than their counterparts in the regular service or

the Volunteer Reserve who were established in business or could afford the life anyway, but again all men who loved flying and the life. Then came the Volunteer Reserve, conceived for rapid expansion of the pilot and navigator establishment necessary for the emergency. They were a very mixed bunch of individuals, from all walks of life and social background, with one common factor – a keenness to fly, either because of their love of flying, or because of the threat of war and a desire to get into it early. Most were either professionally qualified, training to be, or in jobs already and not dependent upon the RAF (VR) for a salary, albeit the weekly attendance money was welcomed, of course. The Auxiliary and VR units were therefore uninhibited, not career-conscious or restricted by the system of procedures, free to express themselves in a common bond: an interest in flying.

Auxiliary squadron 601 (County of London), known as the 'Millionaire's' squadron, was virtually raised in White's Club, St. James's by Lord Edward Grosvenor. The Right Hon. Edward Guest formed 600 squadron (City of London) together with wealthy City contemporaries. With war imminent, the AAF could show 14 squadrons in the line, about a quarter of the strength of Fighter Command. The two Scottish Auxiliaries, 602 (City of Glasgow) and 603 (City of Edinburgh) were in regular action against the enemy from October 1939. By 1940, Sergeant pilots of the RAFVR represented a third of the Command's total strength. 'The Battle of Britain' said Sandy Johnstone, 'established once and for all that members of the Auxiliary and Reserve forces were more than able to play their full part.'

Apprentices' Schools at Halton and elsewhere, trained a number of ground crew who became successful pilots, such as Charles Widdows, a first-rate airman who later attended Cranwell, the entry route for permanent commissions. Another of the College's outstanding cadets was Brian Kingcome, stationed at Hornchurch with 65 Squadron. Kingcome discovered that the Sector Station was 'luxurious beyond belief'. Excursions for lunch were chalked up as flying practice, 'If I wanted to take off and fly up to a friend of mine who had an airfield or station somewhere a hundred miles away for lunch, I would just go.'

OPPOSITE *The Flying Sword: The Story of 601 Squadron*, noted that Edward Grosvenor 'chose his officers from among gentlemen of sufficient means not to be overawed by him, and sufficient means not to be excluded from his favourite pastimes – eating, drinking and White's.' Few 'millionaires' in the auxiliary squadrons survived the war.

BELOW *On test*: Charles Widdows, who test flew production prototypes of both Hurricanes and Spitfires.

The Hornchurch station record book, April 1940, memorably recorded:

> During the last month a determined drive has been made by the Station Commander to make the station a pleasanter and more attractive place. Roads and paths were cleared up and edges whitewashed, grass verges trimmed and lawns cut. A large number of bulbs, plants and rose trees were planted and every squadron and section given tools to cultivate their own part of the camp.

Ken MacKenzie was posted to another Sector Station, Kenley:

> Arriving at Kenley was quite an experience. It was a full peace time RAF station with permanent buildings, good accommodation, very luxurious after my previous postings. My room was in the East Wing with ample room to park the MG outside the back door, most convenient, good beds, clean sheets, a batman to look after one, good food... well, hell, if it was going to be a short life but a hectic one, this was the way to live it!'

Not all stations aspired to such permanence. At Warmwell, in 10 Group, pilots of 609 Squadron were dispersed in a canvas tent prone to blowing down. In the mess, meal hours were strictly observed and thereafter the doors locked, to the frustration of pilots

OPPOSITE *The thin blue line*: officers and NCO pilots of 610 'County of Chester' Squadron 'A' Flight, Hawkinge, July 1940. The life of a fighter pilot at a forward airfield was one of skill, daring and inevitable loss.

BELOW LEFT *Men Like These*: (left to right) Jerzy Jankiewicz, Sir Archibald Hope, Jack Riddle, whose brother Hugh also flew with 601 in the battle, and Bill Clyde, ex-British ski champion. Jankiewicz failed to return from a mission in 1942.

BELOW RIGHT *Wing man*: 601 Squadron pilot Michael Robinson and his damaged Hurricane pose for the camera. The nation thrilled to the exploits of the 'Brylcreem Boys.'

OPPOSITE *'Somewhere in Scotland'*: ran the *Daily Mail* caption. Chess, draughts or cards were common pursuits among pilots waiting at dispersal. 'Telephonitis' said Harold Bird-Wilson, 17 Squadron, 'became a norm, worrying and to some "twitching" on the nerves.'

LEFT *Reading matter*: 19 Squadron Leader Brian Lane (third left), and fellow pilots, lounging in Lloyd Loom chairs at Fowlmere. Lane was posted 'missing' in 1942.

BELOW *Top gun*: 303 Squadron's Josef Frantisek. A portrait, drawn weeks before the Czech pilot was lost on a routine mission, by ex-Royal Flying Corps pilot Cuthbert Orde.

returning from operations. John Dundas, brother of Hugh, remarked that Warmwell 'possessed the chief characteristics of a forward station – action and discomfort'.

Pilots of 14 different nations, including aircrew from the Commonwealth and occupied European countries, played a fundamentally important role in the battle. A total of 2,936 British and Allied airmen were awarded the coveted Battle of Britain clasp to the 1939-45 Star campaign medal for flying at least one authorised sortie with an accredited unit of Fighter Command in the period 10 July to 31 October 1940. Polish, Czech and Canadian squadrons took their full share on the combat-ready roster. The presence of the Polish intake accounted for 20 per cent of enemy aircraft losses.

Czech ace Josef Frantisek who fought in Poland and France before joining 303 (Polish) Squadron flying Hurricanes, was one of the most prolific scorers in the battle before his loss on a routine flight in October. Gerald Batt was impressed by the skill and experience of Polish and Czech pilots, independently-minded, deadly combatants, and with a common hatred of the enemy:

Domagala flew as my number two, which is one of the reasons I'm still alive. He was an instructor at the Polish School of Flying before the war and was a far better pilot than I was. They could hardly speak any English but show 'em a German and they were deadly, the Poles especially. They were ruthless, they would kill every way and any way they could. I don't think the British had quite the same sort of hatred. If they destroyed an aircraft and the pilot jumped out or went in to the sea, it was 'Cheerio, all the best.' But the Poles and the Czechs would finish him off.

Meantime, in America, the *New York Herald Tribune* reported in July that 'Experienced airmen, preferably those with at least 250 flying hours to their credit, would be welcomed by the RAF.' It is generally assumed 11 United States citizens served with the 'Few', exempted from swearing an oath of allegiance to the British Crown.

One of the most celebrated American pilots, who compelled the admiration of fellow pilots in 601 'Millionaire's' Squadron, was Billy Fiske. The son of an international banker in Chicago, Fiske kept fast company, setting the Cambridge to London record in his supercharged Bentley while he was at the University and racing a Stutz, aged 19, at Le Mans. At St.Moritz, he raised the Cresta Run record and, in 1932, captained the winning US Olympic bobsleigh team. In 1938, in a society wedding beloved by the popular press, Fiske married the

BELOW LEFT *One of our airmen*: Fiske and his wife, the former Countess of Warwick. A plaque in St.Paul's Cathedral commemorates 'An American Citizen Who Died That England Might Live.'

former wife of the Earl of Warwick. He volunteered for the RAF two weeks after war was declared.

The commitment of 126 New Zealanders, 99 Canadians, 33 Australians, 25 South Africans, 10 Irish, 3 Rhodesians, a Jamaican and a Newfoundlander brought an imperial dimension to the Battle of Britain. The cost was very high – over 40 per cent of Australian and South African pilots lost their lives during the battle.

Commonwealth pilots were among the best known, and top scoring, airmen in 1940. 'Al' Deere, Colin Gray and Brian Carbury from New Zealand; Australia's Pat Hughes; Johnny Kent, one of the leading Canadians; sharp-shooter 'Sailor' Malan from South Africa, and Ireland's 'Killy' Kilmartin and 'Paddy' Finucane, joined the Battle of Britain roll of honour. In company with their British counterparts – names such as Cunningham, Doe, Dundas, Kingcome, Lacey, Page, Townsend and Stanford Tuck – men like these held the front line of fighter defence. The Battle of Britain was truly a battle of many nations.

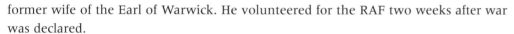
THIS PAGE *Fighter boys*: (left to right) Henri Lafont, 'Ginger' Lacey, 'Sailor' Malan and Johnny Kent.

ASSAULT FROM THE SKY

The Battle of Britain is about to begin. Members of the Royal Air Force, the fate of generations lies in your hands.

H.C.T. DOWDING,
COMMANDER-IN-CHIEF
FIGHTER COMMAND,
8 AUGUST 1940

OPPOSITE *The Third Service*: Hurricanes – quoting 'Johnnie' Johnson – in 'wretched three-plane "vics".' 'Sailor' Malan, among others, adopted more manoeuvrable tactics to meet Me 109s on better terms.

Exactly when the Battle of Britain began is debatable. Various chronologies have been suggested by the former protagonists, but the official British dates are recognized as 10 July to 31 October 1940. In June and July the enemy flew armed reconnaissance missions and sent over formations of bombers and Stukas protected by a fighter screen, which attacked shipping and other targets along the south coast of England. The primary objective remained constant throughout the air conflict: to fight in conditions that favoured the aggressor. 'The means of gaining air superiority' said Theo Osterkamp, commanding fighter units in the Pas de Calais area, 'is the "free hunting" patrol, with the aim of bringing the enemy into action in the air and shooting down as many as possible.'

A fighter squadron of twelve aircraft was divided into two flights. 'A' Flight consisted of three aircraft in Yellow and Red sections, and 'B' Flight the same number of aircraft in Blue and Green sections. Flights were maintained in various sates of preparedness: 'Available' squadrons were ready to be in the air within so many minutes of receiving an order from a Controller to 'scramble'. 'Readiness' reduced this period to a minimum. '"Scrambles" were rapid scrambling into a parachute and into the cockpit,' said Ken MacKenzie, 'hence the name.'

At the start of the ordeal by air the most common Fighter Command formation was the V-shaped 'vic' (the word deriving from the early phonetic alphabet). On sighting the enemy the leader of the first section gave the 'Tally Ho!' and, in theory, ordered one of the prescribed Fighting Area Attacks from astern. In the event, however, pilots keeping tight station in high velocity engagements found themselves 'bounced' by enemy 'snappers' (fighter pilot slang for Me 109s) practised in making the best use of sky, up-sun. 'The sun was most times in our eyes,' said Ivor Cosby. 'We had, however, the advantage of greater time in the air and the psychological advantage of fighting most times over home territory.' In the words of Theo Osterkamp, 'the enemy had to be sought over his own territory'.

ABOVE *High altitude*: Me 109s in formation. Top secret Enigma decrypts of wireless traffic provided insight into German dispositions.

The origins of the *Schwarm*, a loose formation of two pairs of fighters, the leading pair flying to one side, slightly ahead of the second, date from the Spanish Civil War. A highly manoeuvrable formation, popularised by Werner Moelders, one of the Luftwaffe's top scoring aces, the *Schwarm* was known as the 'finger four' to British pilots.

The disconcerting loss rates in the battle due to 'vics', limiting a pilot's radius of action, demanded intensive counter action. New tactics of air fighting, approved by Park in August, included attacks by diving though cloud, the tricky wide-angle deflection shot and the intimidating head-on assault, calling for great ability and plenty of old-fashioned nerve. Gerry Edge, commanding 253 Squadron, was one of its chief exponents:

> They didn't like that head-on attack, you know, but you had to judge the breakaway point right. If you left it to the last 100 yards then you were in trouble due to the fast closing speeds. But once you got the hang of it, the head on attack was a piece of cake. When you opened fire, you'd kill or badly wound the pilot. Then you'd rake the whole line as you broke away. On one attack the first He III hit crashed straight into the next.

Hilary St George Saunders's *The Battle of Britain*, the HMSO's wartime best-seller, painted a timely picture of what Fighter Command had most reason to fear in the highly charged summer of 1940:

> The enemy was by now beginning to realise that our fighter force was considerably stronger than he had imagined. It was evidently time to take drastic action. Our fighters must be put out of commission. Therefore, while still maintaining his attacks on coastal towns, he sent large forces to deal with fighter aerodromes in the South and South-East of England...

On 6 August Goering summoned senior commanders to Karinhall, his sumptuous estate named in memory of his first wife. The plan, said Goering, was concerted action 'to eliminate the English Air Force both as a fighting force and in its ground organisations'. The destruction of aircraft factories, Goering explained, would be completed through bombing by day and night. His belief in sheer force and superior numbers led to extravagantly optimistic claims that the sustained offensive against Fighter Command, clearing the way for a contemplated invasion, would take four days. The operative code-word for the grand assault was *Adlerangriff* (Attack of Eagles).

It is not surprising that defenders lived in daily apprehension of raids against the radar net figuring in the German High Command's assault from the sky. The sharp low-altitude attacks by elite Luftwaffe units on 12 August, the eve of *Adlertag* (Eagle Day), were planned to black-out the RAF's network of warning and control. Chain Home stations were put out of action but with the exception of Ventnor, where essential buildings were destroyed, stations were back on the air within hours. The lattice-work transmitter masts presented – theoretically at least – a conspicuous target, but the towers were resilient to blast and damage was superficial. 'It is doubtful' stated Goering 'whether there is any point in continuing the attacks on radar stations, since not one of those attacked has so far been put out of action.'

This absence of judgement was fully confirmed by the lack of attention paid to CH stations during the battle. In view of the strength and depth of enemy air fleets and the supreme importance of the ground-to-air control system of interception it was a gross error. The governing factor was faulty intelligence: in appraising the situation on 7 August 'Beppo' Schmid, Chief of Luftwaffe

BELOW *Forced-landing*: downed Me 109, Northdown, Kent. 'The English territorial defence is non-existent!' declared Ribbentrop, the German Foreign Minister in September. By this time, the Luftwaffe began to doubt the wisdom that they could achieve command of the air.

Then the move south to help in the defence of London. He had altogether brought down many planes, both here and in France, but was shot down himself in mortal combat on 15 September, after sending to earth a further two enemy planes. His commander said he must have been mortally wounded at the onset as he did not attempt to bale out. The shock and the pain and the grief which followed I cannot dwell upon...
I only know that of all the grief we mortals have to bear, the loss of an only son is the worst.

DIARY OF CONSTANCE MARCHAND,
MOTHER OF ROY MARCHAND,
73 SQUADRON.

Intelligence, informed his air fleet commanders that British fighters were 'tied to their respective ground stations... consequently the assembly of strong fighter forces at determined points and at short notice is not to be expected.' As for the Luftwaffe, a ground-to-air control system was not introduced until two years after the battle. In July 1940 Adolf Galland summed up the situation:

> We realised that R.A.F. fighter formations must be controlled from the ground by some new procedure, because we heard commands skilfully and accurately directing Spitfires and Hurricanes on to German formations. We had no radio fighter control at the time... and no way of knowing what the British were doing with their forces as each battle progressed.

Another irreversible error was underestimation of British fighter production by German Intelligence. Under the January 1940 Harrogate Programme manufacture of 3,602 fighters was planned, but actual production reached 4,283 by the end of the year.

Output of single-engined fighters rose consistently throughout the summer under Churchill's Ministry of Aircraft Production. Manufacture of single-engined fighters during the battle was in fact double that of the German aircraft industry.

Lord Beaverbrook, proprietor of *Express* newspapers, was in charge at the newly-established ministry. One of the Prime Minister's private secretaries described the Canadian tycoon as 'twenty-five per cent thug, fifteen-per cent crook and the remainder a combination of genius and real goodness of heart.' Like Dowding, whose son Derek flew with 74 Squadron in the battle, Beaverbrook had a son, Max, serving in the front line.

Before the war, existing manufacturing plants were nominated as 'shadow factories' in readiness for stepped-up aircraft production when hostilities began. A new, purpose-built 'shadow factory', at Castle Bromwich, near Birmingham, opened in 1938 and, following Beaverbrook's personal intervention, concentrated on Spitfire production. Churchill noted 'a surprising improvement in the supply and repair of aeroplanes' under his old acquaintance.

The date set for *Adlertag* was contingent on favourable weather, and a poor outlook over the English Channel twice forced postponement. The opening of the protracted offensive was inauspicious. At the last minute on the morning of 13 August Goering received a report of thick and unbroken cloud over the target. He sent out another postponement order but the signal did not reach all units in time. A false, and a confused, start yet the Luftwaffe flew almost 1,500 sorties in 24 hours, including an attack on Castle Bromwich. Next morning *The Times* told its readers that pilots of Fighter Command were no longer 'daring young adventurers' but 'Men with a Mission, men who feel a personal responsibility for helping to destroy that threatening machine that is the Luftwaffe.'

It was 15 August before Goering finally launched his day-long offensive. 'Operations' he ordered, 'will be exclusively directed against the enemy Air Force including the enemy aircraft industry...For the moment, other targets should be ignored.' The fiercest day's fighting so far included a heavy raid by *Luftflotte* 5 in the north. German Intelligence had reported that with many squadrons moved south for the defence of London, the north-east coast was ill-defended. The cost of this

ABOVE *Bombing run*: Heinkel He III over the target. 'The fact is that the dropping of bombs from the sky' wrote a French soldier, 'has a unique power of spreading terror.'

OPPOSITE *Olympians*: Max Aitken (extreme right), son of Lord Beaverbrook, and Willie Rhodes-Moorhouse (white overalls), son of the first air VC. Both took part, like Billy Fiske, in the last pre-war Winter Olympics meeting at St.Moritz. Only Aitken survived the war.

mistaken assessment was high in bombers and Me 110s and no further attacks were made from Norway. Churchill called Dowding's policy of keeping fighters stationed in the north 'an example of genius in the art of war'. Luftwaffe losses, 76 aircraft, were the highest yet.

On 16 August, in the company of General Hastings Ismay, Churchill paid one of his several visits to 11 Group headquarters at Uxbridge. 'There had been heavy fighting' wrote Ismay, 'throughout the afternoon, and at one moment every single squadron in the Group was engaged, there was nothing in reserve, and the map table showed new waves of attackers crossing the coast. I felt sick with fear.'

In a heavy raid on Tangmere on the same day, American Billy Fiske's Hurricane was hit by return fire from a Stuka. He forced-landed in flames, suffering burns to the face and hands. The station adjutant who visited him the following day said he was 'perky as hell' but later that day he was dead – seemingly from post-operative shock. Sir Archibald Hope Bt, his commander, wrote:

Unquestionably Billy Fiske was the best pilot I have ever known. It was unbelievable how good he was. He picked up so fast it wasn't true. He'd flown a bit before, but he was a natural fighter pilot. He was also terribly nice and extraordinarily modest, and fitted into the squadron very well.

As the air fleets moved remorselessly into action against the Sector Stations, Kenley came in for attention. On 18 August, between 30 and 50 bombers destroyed hangars and Hurricanes on the ground, and killed nine personnel. All communications on the aerodrome were cut. Anthony Norman was a Kenley Flight Controller:

BELOW *Shot down*: Heinkel pilot Heinz Friedrich (left) and crewman are led away to captivity. The French government agreed to hand over 400 captured pilots before the fall of France. A promise never kept.

We felt we had won a great victory – the Germans had tried very hard to wreck Kenley, but we had survived. And by the late afternoon we were back in business again. If one had spoken to anyone on Kenley that afternoon, one would have found them in the highest of spirits. Nobody in the front line worried too much about the wrecked hangars. Nor the wrecked aircraft; it was merely a case of asking for some more and they would arrive – and they did. So long as the people and the system survived, that was all that mattered. Equipment could be replaced and buildings could be repaired.

The main daylight raids on Fighter Command aerodromes are regarded as the crux of the Battle of Britain. A battle typified by the arena of aerial combat above Churchill's 'highly menaced coastline' and, in the words of the official narrative, 'the fields of Kent and Sussex, the rolling countryside of Hampshire and Dorset, the flat lands of Essex and the sprawling mass of London.'

The 11 Group forward stations at Hawkinge, Lympne and Manston, were prime targets and temporarily put out of action. 'Staff and ground crew worked themselves to the bone to keep their airfields serviceable and aircraft flying' remembered Sandy Johnstone. 'Nothing else mattered…but one wondered how much longer one could go on taking such a hammering.' 'The ground crew, RAF and WAAF, were just marvellous,' said Harold Bird-Wilson, 17 Squadron. 'All maintained our Hurricanes in a most professional manner.' That said, fitters, armourers, signallers and skilled instrument mechanics were in short supply.

Meanwhile, heavy strikes against airfields meant the ever-present threat of unexploded bombs. The testing art of handling UXBs with complex fusing systems and booby-trapped time clocks fell to men like John MacBean. 'No one who has not confronted a bomb with a fuse ticking can ever appreciate the courage and dedication displayed by the Demolition Squads, who with little experience and primitive tools, made a very significant contribution to the Battle of Britain.' In the final weeks of August, over 250 UXBs landed on RAF airfields, excluding bombs recovered from crashed aircraft. The repeated heavy attacks in August led to the introduction of Airfield Servicing Parties for each aerodrome.

BELOW *Height of the battle*: Luftwaffe aerial view of Tangmere and satellites show cratering from bombing runs. The German High Command was confused by conflicting evidence of enemy losses. In August, Fighter Command loss rates were outstripping production and training, yet Dowding had 700 aircraft available. Goering claimed the enemy was virtually beaten.

Elspeth Green was stationed at Biggin Hill:

BELOW LEFT *Section station*: (left) Elspeth C. Henderson (Elspeth Green), passes a bomb damaged Biggin Hill, October 1940. 'I had known the extremes of fear, friendship and of fun' she wrote of her time at the 11 Group station.

BELOW RIGHT *High octane*: armourers at work. Hurricanes and Spitfires switched from 87 octane fuel to the potent 'rich mixture response' 100 octane, increasing combat rating, rate of climb and maximum speed.

I remember thinking, 'What an odd name and where an earth is it?' When someone said that it was near London, I thought that wouldn't be too bad – little did I know! At first we did not have uniforms, just shirts with any skirt we happened to have. On duty at night we slept under the table. . . until a rest room and shelter were built.

On 30 August the Luftwaffe tried very hard to wreck Biggin Hill. No air-raid warning was given and in a devastatingly effective bombing run by Ju 88s, flying at less than a thousand feet, a WAAF shelter received a direct hit and 39 were killed – the single largest loss of life during the battle. Elspeth Green was in the thick of it on that day:

LEFT *Enemy coast ahead*: Me 110 propaganda photograph. In September, Galland told Goering 'British plane wastage was far lower and production far higher than the German intelligence staff estimated and now events were exposing the error so plainly that it had to be acknowledged.'

It was on a Friday that the Operations Room was destroyed. I was on duty and remember how I felt as we dived under table and desks for cover. It was a kind of detached curiosity – 'this is me and this is happening to me' – somewhat selfish thoughts. Work and actual danger were never the worst, the worst was the anticipation...time to worry about families at home.

And Dowding was running short of pilots fit to fight: Fighter Command experienced an unsustainable loss rate of 22 per cent of its full establishment during August and he later reported, in a characteristically acute assessment, that:

By the beginning of September the incidence of casualties became so serious that a fresh squadron would become depleted and exhausted before any of the resting

The standard officer's Van Heusen collar shrank in contact with sea water and was, therefore very dangerous if you went in the drink. Several pilots were throttled and drowned. The silk scarf was the answer. The ten days in France was hell, a real killer. The Battle of Britain was a picnic compared. I used to pass on the lessons we learned in France. 'Get in close' was probably the most important. 'You must get right in close to kill.' Another was, 'Make sure your cockpit is ready. Check everything, especially the hood runners.'

W.D.DAVID, 87 AND 213 SQUADRONS

and re-forming squadrons were ready to take its place. Fighter pilots were no longer being produced in numbers sufficient to fill the gaps in the fighting ranks.

Pilots were transferred from other Commands after brief conversion periods, final training was cut from a month to a fortnight, and a rotation system was introduced to relieve increasingly hard-pressed squadrons. The Luftwaffe kept up the pressure: squadrons of ten or twelve found themselves engaging close formations of 20 to 40 bombers screened by more than a 100 fighters. Sheer weight of numbers meant that the enemy broke through the forward fighter screen to reach their objectives. 'The scales had tilted against Fighter Command' wrote Churchill.

In these circumstances, the effects of a mounting number of nerve-racking daily sorties and the stresses of high-altitude combat were felt severely. The 'Few' were under considerable strain. Sandy Johnstone was of them:

> We soon adapted to the ever increasing pressures of being in action three, four and sometimes five times a day, occasionally losing one's closest colleagues in the process and never able to relax for a moment. However, fatigue soon took its toll and it was not uncommon for the lads to fall asleep as soon as they returned to dispersals, only to be rudely awakened by their Intelligence Officers demanding details of their actions for their Combat Reports, or to be ordered into the air again to meet a fresh attack. On one occasion a Hurricane landed back at base and stopped at the end of its run, whereupon the Rescue Services assumed its pilot had been wounded in combat and rushed to his aid, only to discover him fast asleep in the cockpit.

Denis Robinson was flying with 152 Squadron:

> Many of our friends had been killed. In my squadron, of the 22 pilots at the beginning of the battle, 12 of them were killed. Many of the pilots who replaced them were also killed. We cared more about our aircraft than people and were commended for the number of enemy aircraft we destroyed, given medals and

---

Although a day-fighter squadron, circumstances demanded that we should make some attempt at continuing our activities into the night, and attempt it was. Of the many night patrols we made between June and August only one, so far as I can remember, achieved success. Alan Wright not only saw something, but effectively shot at it. For most of us it was a case of showing the flag to the locals, who no doubt got some satisfaction out of hearing a couple of Spitfires screaming overhead, even if the successes were brought about by our endeavours to get out of our own searchlights and subsequent A.A. fire.

TREVOR WADE, 92 SQUADRON

OPPOSITE *Battle Over Britain, 1940*: by C.F. 'Bunny' Currant, 605 Squadron. Fighter Command lost more aircraft in the crucial fortnight before 7 September than it could replace from repair and manufacture. After the start of the Blitz replacements well exceeded losses.

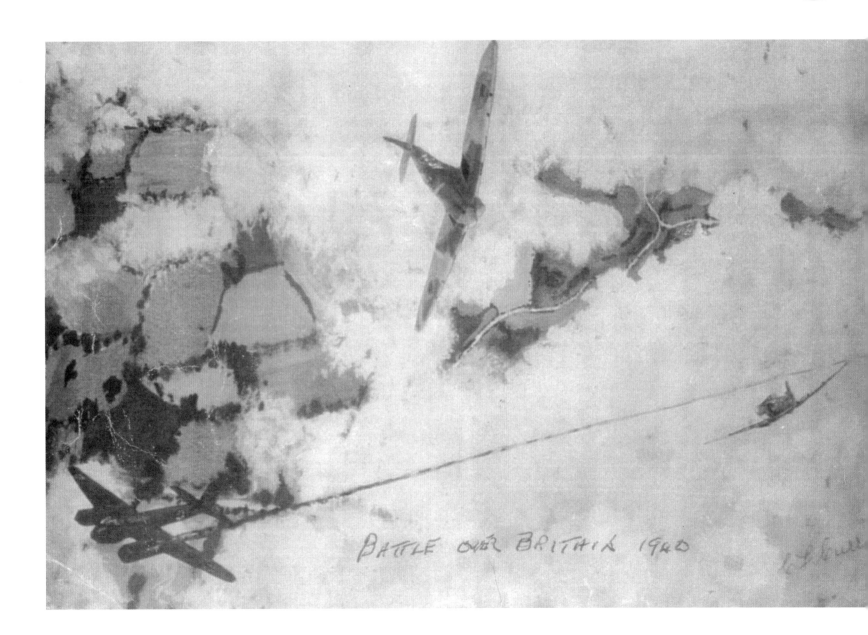

BATTLE OVER BRITAIN 1940

ABOVE *The Reckoning*: operations board, War Cabinet Headquarters. Both sides grossly exaggerated the other's losses and their own victories. Double- or treble-counting by pilots reporting the same victims was a prime example of the fog of war.

looked upon as heroes. We had killed and maimed German airmen. During the battle I flew 60 operational sorties against the enemy from June to September, when I was relieved. By this time I felt utterly drained and exhausted, was probably given a rest just in time. My value system had changed and youth had gone. I was 22 years old.

The vital search in the air was for 'the enemy unseen'. Alex Ingle's Hurricane was 'bounced' by a Me 109:

Immediately I took evasive action by diving into cloud beneath me, whereupon my engine seized and black oil covered the windscreen...

On looking at the starboard wing, I noticed a large hole with two jagged ends of wire protruding from it... The aircraft had been hit by cannon shell and machine-gun bullets from below. The aileron controls were severed, the air speed indicator damaged, the oil and hydraulic pipe fractured, and, of course, the engine seized.

Ingle forced-landed and escaped, remarkably, with minor injury. When Ralph Hope's Hurricane was shot down he 'took to the silk':

Saturday was not quite such a success from my point of view, as on our third patrol I lost my aircraft. We were at about 21,000ft when we got involved with a squadron of Me 109s. They got me before I even saw them, which is very annoying. I first felt a kind of funny bump, and as I turned to see what was up, my controls suddenly felt funny, a lot of red sparks and black smoke appeared round my feet and a cloud of white smoke, probably glycol, began streaming back from the engine. The aircraft began going downhill fast. I slid back the hood and began to get out... The air seized hold of me and there was a wrench as my oxygen tube snapped off (I had forgotten to undo it) and I shot out into the sky. The aeroplane disappeared. It was nice and cool falling. I was head down, of course, but found the position quite comfortable, there was no sense of speed or feeling of falling.

Free of the aircraft, he floated 'oh! so slowly earthwards' to land unhurt atop an oak tree. Hope, a cousin of Neville Chamberlain, was killed in October, stalking a Heinkel 111 over home defences. The Operations Record Book of 605 'County of Warwick' Squadron recorded: 'Apart from being the only original 605 Squadron auxiliary still in the squadron, his charming personality and quiet sense of humour and stability will be much missed by everyone in the squadron.'

A brave and skilful pilot was capable of out-turning his pursuer. Here is Geoffrey Wellum in *First Light:*

> If you want to shake someone off your tail you have to fly your Spitfire to its limits. In a tight turn you increase the G loading to such an extent that the wings

So don't worry, we are going to win this war even if we have only one aeroplane and one pilot left – the Boche could produce the whole Luftwaffe and you would see the one pilot and the one aeroplane go into combat. All that sounds very involved, but I am trying to convey to you something of the spirit of 'Per ardua ad astra' today. The spirit of the average pilot has to be seen to be believed.

RONALD WIGHT, 213 SQUADRON, LETTER TO HIS MOTHER

LEFT *'Nick'*: James Nicholson and family after receiving his VC. Nicholson's Hurricane, leading 254 Squadron near Southampton on 16 August, was hit by enemy fire. A mass of flame, he was ready to bale out when, in the words of the *London Gazette*, 'he sighted an enemy fighter. This he attacked and shot down although as a result of staying in his burning aircraft, he sustained serious burns...' Fighter Command's only VC did not survive the war.

can no longer support the weight and the plane stalls, with momentary loss of control. However, in a Spitfire, just before the stall, the whole aircraft judders, it's a stall warning if you like. With practice and experience you could hold the plane on this judder in a very tight turn. You never actually stall the aircraft and you don't need to struggle to regain control because you never lose it. A 109 can't stay with you.

On 29 August Kesselring's fighter commander informed his chief that 'unlimited fighter superiority' had been achieved. German Air Intelligence, hopelessly wide of the mark, reported that Fighter Command had lost 50 per cent of its fighter force, against a loss

RIGHT *Hardest Day*: a Stuka's final dive, near Chichester, 18 August, thereafter known as 'The Hardest Day.' RAF pilots showed great courage in overcoming fear and hazarding their lives. 'I didn't really think of having any fear at the time' said Ben Bowring, 111 Squadron, 'What had overcome it was a desire to get one's own back for everything done to your friends.'

OPPOSITE *A path to the sky*: 'We just went ploughing in' said Harold Bird-Wilson, 'picked a target and fought. Shots of adrenalin and dryness of mouth. The natural worry of life and death.'

ABOVE *Tail-piece*: Squadron trophy. By the end of October, the Luftwaffe had lost around 1,800 aircraft. Fighter Command loss estimates by the enemy were blindly optimistic; more aircraft were reported shot down than actually existed.

OPPOSITE *Night Blitz*: spotters on the roof of Northcliffe House, the *Daily Mail* building. London was raided by up to 400 bombers virtually every night until mid-November, causing widespread destruction and heavy civilian casualties.

rate of only 12 per cent of Luftwaffe fighters. The vastly inflated figures masked the true picture: fighter losses on both sides were almost identical during August. At a conference in the Hague on 3 September, Goering announced plans for a massive air strike on London. Sperrle was unconvinced, insisting that 'the English still have a thousand fighters available.' Kesselring believed that 'the English have next to nothing left', claiming that 'recently only the bad weather had prevented his bombers from reaching their targets.' Mass daylight raids over London, declared Goering, would force Fighter Command to commit 'its last Spitfires and Hurricanes.'

This was the decisive argument. On 7 September a force of 372 bombers and 642 fighters attacked London. The capital shuddered under two concentrated waves of attack in quick succession. The massively destructive raids smashed structures to atoms and caused fierce conflagrations in the docks of the East End, providing an unmistakable objective for the 255 bombers which attacked after dark. 'It was burning all down the river. It was a horrid sight' said Park, adding, 'Thank God for that because I realised that the methodical Germans had at last switched the attack from my vital aerodromes on to cities.' 'Cromwell' – the code-name for 'Invasion Imminent' – was issued that evening, bringing the Home Forces to a high state of readiness.

The change of strategy was a fateful step. Sandy Johnstone, echoing Park, said 'it allowed the fighter defences that vital breathing space to recover their full potential. From then on, the writing was on the wall for the Luftwaffe.' Night bombing continued on London but the air supremacy needed for 'Sea Lion' could only be achieved by costly daylight raids.

At this stage of the battle the controversial 'Big Wings' debate came to the fore. Douglas Bader, flying with 12 Group adjoining Park's 11 Group, sought to deploy big formations to provide maximum striking power against the enemy. The Duxford Wing, supported by Bader's commander Leigh-Mallory, comprised three or more squadrons flying together under Bader's leadership. Park strongly dismissed his 'Big Wings' theory on the grounds that assembling large formations allowed attacking bombers to reach targets before fighters could intercept them. The controversy rolled on throughout the autumn, exacerbating relations between Park and Leigh-Mallory. 'Big Wings' stated Park, 'would have lost the Battle of London.'

Sunday 15 September, since known as Battle of Britain Day, marked the climax of the air offensive. Goering sent over the strongest escort of the battle – five fighters for every bomber – in a last throw to neutralise Fighter Command. The attack set the seal on the Luftwaffe's eventual retreat: enemy formations were intercepted almost as soon as they crossed the Channel and broken up. One-third of the bomber force was shot down by a scale of effort the Luftwaffe had not expected, nor could match in battle. 'The most

I don't think any of us (and I was older than most) really appreciated the seriousness of the situation. When we could be scared to death five or six times a day and yet find ourselves drinking in the local pub before closing time on a summer evening, it all seemed unreal.'

'MINNIE' MANTON, 56 SQUADRON

brilliant and fruitful of any fought upon a large scale up to that date by the fighters of the Royal Air Force' Churchill told the House of Commons. The War Diary of the German Naval Staff recorded that 'The enemy air force is still by no means defeated; on the contrary, it shows increasing activity.' Two days after Battle of Britain Day, Hitler postponed 'Sea Lion' indefinitely.

London remained the principal target. The 'Blitz' continued for another six weeks and charred ruins of bombed-out buildings became a familiar sight for Londoners. However,

BELOW LEFT *Read all about it*: Londoners took to shelters during the Blitz, including guests of the Savoy Hotel, who provided 'an exceedingly good shelter, below ground, the ceiling reinforced with a regular spider's web of steel struts'.

BELOW RIGHT *Remains of the day*: a stricken Luftwaffe aircraft pictured a few metres from the site of the Battle of Britain Monument on the Embankment.

the assault was maintained mostly by high-flying fighter-bombers. When the threat of invasion had passed and heavy daylight raiding had been abandoned, the balance moved more and more in favour of the defenders. By 31 October, the official end of the air assault, a certain and complete defensive triumph had been achieved. The price was very high: 544 airmen had lost their lives in the Battle of Britain. A necessary battle that is an enduring tribute to the spirit and character of Royal Air Force Fighter Command. Their service and their sacrifices deserve to be remembered.

BELOW *Journey's End*: the Luftwaffe bomber fleets were no match for defending fighters and proved incapable of delivering a knock-out blow. In a fateful step, Hitler, as Churchill had foreseen, turned his sights on Soviet Russia.

AFTER THE BATTLE

We are the Trustees of each other. We do well to remember that the privilege of dying for one's country is not equal to the privilege of living for it.

SIR ARCHIBALD MCINDOE

OPPOSITE *'The Battle of Britain'*: Paul Nash (1889-1946). Official War Artist in both the First and Second World Wars, Nash captures the realities of aerial combat to striking effect. 'You knew' wrote Virginia Cowles, 'the fate of civilisation was being decided fifteen thousand fleet above your head in a world of sun, wind and sky.'

Aircrew in the Battle of Britain were vulnerable to a new disease, a disease of wartime which no other could equal as a therapeutic problem or cause of subsequent disability, a disease known as 'Airman's Burn.' In the years between 1940 and 1945, 4,500 burned aircrew were rescued by reserve squads from wrecked aeroplanes, or parachuted like a blazing torch from stricken aircraft. Of that number, 3,600 sustained burns on the hands (80 per cent of all RAF burns involved the hands) and of the face.

Many of these very young men found themselves at the Maxillo-Facial Unit of the Queen Victoria Hospital, East Grinstead, under the care of Archibald (later Sir Archibald) McIndoe. The most severe cases were admitted to a hut known as Ward Three, and found themselves looking up through the remains of their charred eyelids at the sympathetic face of 'The Boss' or 'Maestro', known to his friends as Archie.

Ann Standen was a wartime nurse in the Burns Unit at East Grinstead:

> It would be wrong to say we weren't horrified. Inwardly, you'd say, 'Oh my God, what will they do with them?' You didn't recoil in horror but you wondered what could be done. Faces were just horrible – even the man I would later marry. By the time he called a halt to the treatment and said enough was enough, he had new eyelids, a new nose, new lips. They couldn't do much with his hands because they were too badly burned. It was amazing what they did do. He had sixty operations. Relatives of the patients would come to the hospital to see the men. Some took it well. Some didn't. It was a shock.

McIndoe set the agenda:

> It is my practice to describe to the patient the scheme to be followed, announce the exact number of operations it will entail, how many weeks or months will be spent

ABOVE *'Maestro'*: Archibald (later Sir Archibald) McIndoe gave everything to the service of a country at war.

OPPOSITE *Fighter pilot*: Geoffrey Page (second from left) briefs pilots before a sortie into Germany. Like many young men of his time, Geoffrey Page formed an early passion to fly. He was rated as an exceptional pilot and returned to operational flying with distinction later in the war.

in hospital and how much time will be required out of hospital to recuperate, what the patient should do during these off-periods and finally, the approximate date when the face will be complete. Only then can his confidence and, above all, his intelligent interest be maintained, for, assuming that in addition a pair of badly burned hands must be restored, the total period of incapacity may be four years.'

Among the first of 'The Few' to be admitted to East Grinstead was Geoffrey Page, who returned to operational flying in a distinguished war and post-war career; Richard Hillary, author of the best-selling *The Last Enemy*, and the CO of 253 Squadron, Tom Gleave:

I heard a metallic click above the roar of my engine...a sudden burst of heat struck my face, and I looked down into the cockpit. A long spout of flame was issuing from the hollow starboard wing root...I had some crazy notion that if I rocked the aircraft and skidded, losing speed, the fire might go out. Not a bit of it; the flames increased until the cockpit was like the centre of a blow-lamp nozzle. There was nothing to do but bale out.'

Archibald Hector McIndoe, born in New Zealand in 1900, was marked out as a surgeon of great ability and perception. His cousin was Sir Harold Gillies, the elder statesman of plastic surgery, who had pioneered work on blasted and burned patients in the first world war. McIndoe joined Gillies in practice in Harley Street, London and his exceptional talents enjoyed an ever-widening reputation. In 1938 he succeeded Gillies as Civilian Consultant in Plastic Surgery to the RAF. The following year, arriving at East Grinstead, he wrote to his mother, 'It is a nice hospital on the outskirts of a nice little town and I think something can be made of it.' His objective was 'the return of the injured person to the community as an economically independent member of that community'. Under his influence, latent hostility to 'service intruders' gave way to a communal desire to understand. East Grinstead became 'the town that didn't stare.'

   McIndoe defined the meticulous craft of cutting, grafting, stitching and reconstituting which he had learned so painstakingly as 'the art of ordinary surgery raised to the *nth* degree of finesse'. The increasing vehemence of the Battle of Britain threw into high relief the urgent need for skilled plastic surgeons: burns from blazing aviation fuel went deep, with the potential for disfigurement and loss of function if not grafted early.

Tom Gleave wrote of his first time on the operating trolley:

> From that moment I started to accumulate a debt that mounted daily, and still mounts; a debt I can never repay, against which human thanks seem utterly inadequate. Every time I see a nurse or doctor now I feel a hidden sense of

'This is Pilot Officer Page, sir. A new arrival.'

Archie McIndoe looked at me over the top of his horn-rimmed spectacles. 'We've met before.'

I smiled. Somehow I always felt happier when talking to McIndoe. 'Yes, sir, at the Royal Masonic Hospital.'

The surgeon bent over my crippled hands, turning them over slowly as he examined the damage. Without raising his head he looked up over his glasses. 'Long job, I'm afraid.'

Hesitantly I asked, 'you'll have to operate?'

This time his head went back and the dark eyes met mine firmly. 'Yes. Many times I'm afraid. But you'll be all right in the end.'

I believed him.

GEOFFREY PAGE, *SHOT DOWN IN FLAMES*

RIGHT *Ward at East Grinstead*: 'the town that did not stare.' A majority of Fighter Command injuries were burns to the hands and face. Pilots experienced a rooted dread of being trapped in a flaming aircraft.

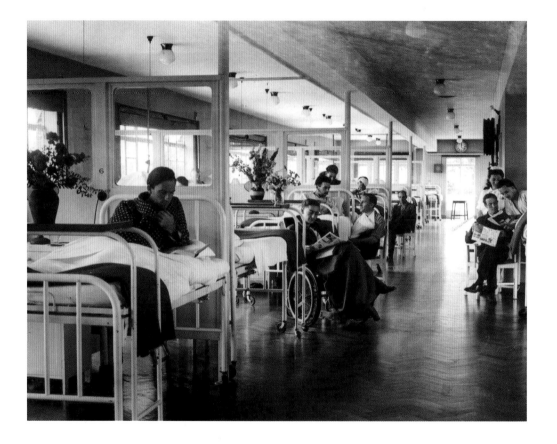

humility, prompted not only by the ceaseless care and attention I received and still receive from them, but also what I saw them do for others far worse than myself, all but dead casualties who have become living miracles.

Patients at East Grinstead, encouraged to witness operations on fellow aircrew, became well-informed on current surgical practice. However, trying to persuade a badly burned airman, the age of a university graduate or younger, with all the normal instincts of a young man, of the merits of occupational therapy in the form of basket making or embroidery could produce, in the words of one eye-witness, 'quite shattering despair, disillusionment, indifference and profanity – no matter how charming the therapist.'

The answer to this problem came from McIndoe, who sought the help of industry. Reid and Sigrist, aircraft instrument makers, were approached to set up a small satellite factory in the hospital grounds. It is worth remarking that in the first year, production per man-hour exceeded the parent factory, and the rejection rate of tested instruments was the lowest recorded. Like Dowding and his 'chicks', nothing was too good for McIndoe's 'Pigs.'

In 1941, the RAF patients formed a club, originally 'The Maxillonians', a title soon replaced by 'The Guinea Pigs.' Geoffrey Page was a founding member:

It was during these early days in the hospital that a small group of us started a club that is now world famous. With the original idea of forming it as a drinking club, it was soon to change its nature, although the basic premise has always been the same. The Guinea Pig Club formed its first meeting in a small hut between the wooden wartime wards, over glasses of beer, and sherry. Why the name 'Guinea Pig?' It started as a joke by us on our brilliant surgical team of Archibald McIndoe, Jill Mullins and John Hunter. One of the founder members had a very attractive wife, who was also a superb artist. At our request she came into the ward one morning and drew a beautiful sketch of a guinea pig on her husband's chest before he went off to the operating room. We knew that once on the table the surgical gown would be removed, revealing the drawing. As both the medicos and ourselves were fully aware that we were to an extent pioneers in the modern techniques of skin grafting, it was right and proper we should send our message of being 'Guinea Pigs' to our medical partners. At our first meeting we

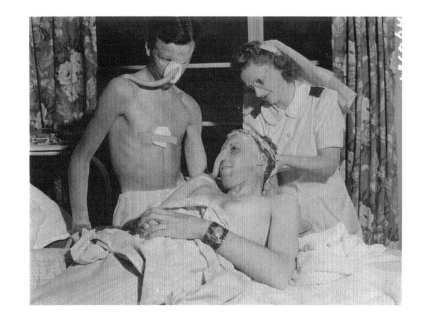

BELOW *Recovery*: William Foxley and Stu Duncan after reconstructive surgery, with Sister Stapleford at East Grinstead.

collected a modest entrance fee, and put the monies into the safe keeping of our elected treasurer. He had been unanimously elected, as his burnt legs were in plaster, and he was therefore incapable of running away with the club funds. At our second meeting I proposed that we should extend our activities beyond those of pouring large quantities of liquid down our throats. My suggestion was that those of us who could return to a useful life should ensure that our less fortunate members should be looked after by us financially.

Archie McIndoe was elected President of the club, surgeons and scientists appointed honorary members, and benefactors accommodated by the formation of the Society for the Prevention of Cruelty to Guinea Pigs.

Treatment of burned aircrew brought out all that was best in Mcindoe: his artistic surgical skill, his dynamic personality, tireless energy and deep-rooted humanity. He understood that physical repair was only half the job – incomplete without full mental and moral rehabilitation:

Eventually there comes the exciting moment when all the tissue required in the repair of an injured face is in position, all major contraction has been overcome and the patient has resolved his scars, softened his grafts, and is ready for trimming. The aim is to produce a face which in sum total is symmetrical in its separate parts, of good colour and texture and freely mobile so that expression of mood is possible in all its infinite variety. It is not possible to construct a face from one destroyed of which the observer is unconscious, but it should not leave in his mind an impression of repulsion and the patient himself should not be an object of remark or pity. Only then can the surgeon feel that his work has been faithfully done.

Just before his unexpected death in 1960, McIndoe had confided to one of his young surgeons that 'the next great era in surgery will be when we learn how to transplant tissue from one person to another'. He saw the day when 'whole limbs, kidneys, lungs and even hearts will be surgically replaced'.

A colleague wrote at the time of his death of his 'imperishable contribution to victory in the darkest days of this country's history', another spoke of his 'congregation of friends more embracing than most'. One of his Guinea Pigs said, 'no matter how bad things were, he always made them better'. If ever a man can be said to have given his heart to a collection of buildings, Archie McIndoe gave his to the Queen Victoria Hospital.

He was, in the words of Sir Harold Gillies, 'truly one of the great heroes of the Battle of Britain'.

Today, the Blond McIndoe Research Centre, building on the outstanding achievements of Sir Archibald McIndoe, is a world leader in wound healing. The Centre's Nerve Regeneration Group, based at the University of Manchester, and the Blond McIndoe Research Laboratories, continuing the East Grinstead tradition at the Queen Victoria NHS Trust (QVH), offer unrivalled standards of excellence in the progress of nerve regeneration, wound healing and tissue reconstruction. Sir Archibald McIndoe would have approved.

ABOVE *Faces from the Fire*: two portraits of 'The Boss' with his beloved 'Guinea Pigs'. Reunions, including 'Lost Weekends' were memorable events.

Battle of Britain

What did we earth-bound make of it? A tangle
Of vapour trails, a vertiginously high
Swarming of midges, most a fiery angel
Hurled out of heaven was all we could descry.

How could we know the agony and pride
That scrawled these fading signatures up there,
And the cool expertise of them who died
Or lived through that delirium of the air?

Grounded on history now, we re-enact
Such lives, such deaths. Time laughing out of court
The newspaper heroics and the faked
Statistics leaves us only to record.

What was, what might have been, fighter and bomber,
The tilting sky, tense moves and counterings,
Those who outlived that legendary summer;
Those who went down, its sunlight on their wings.

And You unborn then, what will you make of it
This shadow play of battles long ago?
Be sure of this: they pushed to the uttermost limit
Their luck, skill, nerves. And they were young – like You.

CECIL DAY LEWIS

LEFT *Pilots all*: (left to right) John Cunningham, Paddy Barthropp, Hugh Dundas, Geoffrey Page, Harold Bird-Wilson and (in cockpit) Brian Kingcome. Sotheby's sale, Hendon, September 1990, in support of Blond McIndoe. Photo by Lord Lichfield.

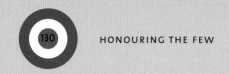

ROLL OF HONOUR

In compiling the list of aircrew who flew in the Battle of Britain and whose names appear on the Monument a mass of documentary material was examined. We have made much use of RAF sources and the Public Record Office in seeking to trace airmen entitled to wear the Battle of Britain clasp. We are also indebted to the late Bruce Burton, the late John Holloway, Edward McManus, Ken Wynn and J.R. Young, AFC, Battle of Britain Fighter Association.

GREAT BRITAIN

Sgt. H H ADAIR
F/O D A ADAMS
Sgt. E H ADAMS
P/O H C ADAMS
F/Lt. J S ADAMS
Sgt. R T ADAMS
AC1 W N ADDISON
P/O R A C AEBERHARDT
F/O N le C AGAZARIAN
AC2 C R AINDOW
Sgt. E D AINGE
AC1 S AINSWORTH
Sgt. A AITKEN
Sgt. H A AITKEN
S/Ldr. J W M AITKEN
P/O H J AKROYD
Sgt. A V ALBERTINI
P/O E S ALDOUS
P/O F J ALDRIDGE
P/O K R ALDRIDGE
P/O A J M ALDWINCKLE
Sgt. E A ALEXANDER
P/O J W E ALEXANDER
F/Lt. G ALLARD
P/O P O D ALLCOCK
P/O H R ALLEN
F/O J L ALLEN
Sgt. J W ALLEN
Sgt. K M ALLEN

Sgt. L H ALLEN
Sgt. H H ALLGOOD
Sgt. J W ALLISON
S/Ldr. H G L ALLSOP
Sgt. L C ALLTON
P/O C F AMBROSE
P/O R AMBROSE
Sgt. C ANDERSON
P/O D J ANDERSON
Sgt. J A ANDERSON
AC1 J D ANDERSON
S/Ldr. M F ANDERSON
F/O C J D ANDREAE
Sgt. S ANDREW
P/O S E ANDREWS
Sgt. J C C ANGUS
Sgt. R A ANGUS
P/O M J APPLEBY
P/O A N R L APPLEFORD
Sgt. I K ARBER
P/O P W ARBON
Sgt. J ARBUTHNOT
Sgt. H T ARCHER
Sgt. S ARCHER
P/O E W ARIES
F/Lt. D L ARMITAGE
Sgt. J F ARMITAGE
F/O W ARMSTRONG
Sgt. S J ARNFIELD
P/O C J ARTHUR

F/Lt. R C V ASH
Sgt. A E ASHCROFT
F/Lt. G ASHFIELD
P/O D G ASHTON
Sgt. D K ASHTON
Sgt. J ASHWORTH
Sgt. A T R ASLETT
Sgt. D J ASLIN
P/O W R ASSHETON
Sgt. F P J ATKINS
P/O A A ATKINSON
Sgt. G ATKINSON
P/O G B ATKINSON
P/O H D ATKINSON
F/Lt. M R ATKINSON
P/O R ATKINSON
LAC A L AUSTIN
Sgt. A T AUSTIN
F/O F AUSTIN
Sgt. S AUSTIN
Sgt. D H AYERS
Sgt. C A H AYLING
Sgt. C F BABBAGE
P/O J H BACHMANN
F/O C H BACON
Sgt. D H BADDELEY
S/Ldr. D R S BADER
F/Sgt. I J BADGER
S/Ldr. J V C BADGER
AC2 C C BAILEY

P/O G G BAILEY
Sgt. G J BAILEY
P/O H N D BAILEY
P/O J C L D BAILEY
F/O J R A BAILEY
P/O P A BAILLON
P/O G S P BAIN
S/Ldr. C E J BAINES
Sgt. A C BAKER
Sgt. B BAKER
F/O C C M BAKER
Sgt. E D BAKER
F/O H C BAKER
Sgt. L V BAKER
Sgt. R D BAKER
P/O S BAKER
F/Lt. G E BALL
Sgt. C S BAMBERGER
F/O J J F H BANDINEL
S/Ldr. A J BANHAM
Sgt. T H BANISTER
Sgt. W H BANKS
Sgt. E S BANN
P/O F H R BARALDI
P/O R H BARBER
F/O R G A BARCLAY
Sgt. F J BARKER
P/O G L BARKER
Sgt. J K BARKER
Sgt. E C BARNARD

F/Lt. J G C BARNES
Sgt. L D BARNES
F/O W BARNES
S/Ldr. R E BARNETT
P/O R V BARON
Sgt. R G V BARRACLOUGH
Sgt. S M BARRACLOUGH
F/Lt. P H BARRAN
Sgt. W E BARRETT
Sgt. N P G BARRON
Sgt. H J R BARROW
F/O P P C BARTHROPP
Sgt. L H BARTLETT
F/O A C BARTLEY
P/O A R H BARTON
P/O E G BARWELL
W/Cdr. P R BARWELL
Sgt. H BASHFORD
P/O F B BASSETT
P/O G H BATCHELOR
Sgt. L G BATT
Sgt. S BAXTER
Sgt. E A BAYLEY
P/O D BAYLISS
Sgt. E J BAYLISS
F/Lt. A W A BAYNE
S/Ldr. D W BAYNE
F/O G T BAYNHAM
F/Lt. J M BAZIN
F/Lt. S H BAZLEY

Sgt. R BEAMISH
F/O R P BEAMONT
Sgt. J M B BEARD
Sgt. R A BEARDSLEY
Sgt. M A BEATTY
F/Lt. S G BEAUMONT
P/O W BEAUMONT
F/O H J S BEAZLEY
Sgt. E H BEE
Sgt. A F BEECHEY
Sgt. C S F BEER
Sub/Lt.(FAA) H W BEGGS
S/Ldr. L G BELCHEM
P/O C A BELL
Sgt. C H BELL
Sgt. D BELL
F/O J S BELL
Sgt. R BELL
F/O D B BELL-SALTER
Sgt. H J BELL-WALKER
Sgt. G W BENN
Sgt. H E BENNETT
P/O G R BENNETTE
P/O G H BENNIONS
P/O J G BENSON
P/O N J V BENSON
Sgt. B BENT
F/Lt. H R A BERESFORD
Sgt. T C E BERKLEY
Sgt. H W W BERRIDGE

Sgt. A BERRY
F/Sgt. F G BERRY
P/O R BERRY
Sgt. R C BERWICK
Sgt. C BEVERIDGE
F/Lt. M L ff BEYTAGH
Sgt. N BICKNELL
S/Ldr. L C BICKNELL
P/O E G BIDGOOD
Sgt. I K J BIDGOOD
S/Ldr. A J BIGGAR
Sgt. J E BIGNELL
Sgt. A E BINHAM
F/O C N BIRCH
Lt.(FAA) R A BIRD
F/O H A C BIRD-WILSON
P/O T BIRKETT
Mid.(FAA) M A BIRRELL
P/O J D BISDEE
P/O D L BISGOOD
S/Ldr. E R BITMEAD
Sgt. A BLACK
Sgt. H E BLACK
F/Lt. W F BLACKADDER
S/Ldr. G D M BLACKWOOD
F/Lt. C E BLAIR
F/Lt. K H BLAIR
Sub/Lt.(FAA) A G BLAKE
P/O J W BLAND
AC2 W H BLANE
F/O A J BLAYNEY
Sgt. F BLENKHARN
F/O D H BLOMELEY
Sgt. E BLOOR
Sgt. K L O BLOW
Sgt. M C B BODDINGTON
P/O C A W BODIE
F/Lt. D P A BOITEL-GILL
Sgt. H A BOLTON
P/O P V BOOT

AC2 F BOOTH
Sgt. G B BOOTH
Sgt. J J BOOTH
P/O R J BORET
Sgt. R A BOSWELL
F/O R J E BOULDING
F/Lt. J C BOULTER
F/Lt. J E BOULTON
F/Lt. C E BOWEN
P/O N G BOWEN
P/O P D BOWEN
Sgt. H BOWEN-MORRIS
Sgt. O R BOWERMAN
Sgt. L D BOWMAN
F/O B H BOWRING
S/Ldr. A H BOYD
F/O A D McN BOYD
F/Lt. R F BOYD
Sgt. C BOYLE
F/O J R D BRAHAM
Sub-Lt.(FAA) H G K BRAMAH
F/O G R BRANCH
Sgt. G B BRASH
Sgt. R A BREEZE
F/O C P N BRETT
P/O J BREWSTER
Sgt. D R BRIGGS
P/O M F BRIGGS
F/O V M BRIGHT
Sgt. G W BRIMBLE
Sgt. J J BRIMBLE
F/O A W N BRITTON
P/O H W A BRITTON
W/Cdr. H BROADHURST
P/O J W BROADHURST
F/Lt. R E P BROOKER
Sgt. P W BROOM
F/Lt. P M BROTHERS
Sgt. A E BROWN
P/O A W BROWN

Sgt. C B BROWN
Sgt. C W D BROWN
F/O D M BROWN
F/Sgt. F S BROWN
F/Lt. G A BROWN
Sgt. J W BROWN
F/O M P BROWN
P/O N McH BROWN
F/O R C BROWN
P/O R J W BROWN
AC2 R S BROWN
Sgt. C BROWNE
P/O D O M BROWNE
F/Lt. D C BRUCE
Sgt. N BRUMBY
P/O G C BRUNNER
Mid.(FAA) R F BRYANT
F/O L T BRYANT-FENN
P/O J BUCHANAN
P/O J R BUCHANAN
Sgt. J A BUCK
Sgt. J S BUCKNOLE
F/Lt. G O BUDD
F/Lt. C H BULL
P/O J C BULL
Sub/Lt.(FAA) G G R BULMER
Sgt. R F BUMSTEAD
Sgt. D C BUNCH
Sub/Lt.(FAA) S H BUNCH
Sgt. A G BURDEKIN
Sgt. J H B BURGESS
P/O E BURGOYNE
Sgt. P S BURLEY
F/Sgt. F P BURNARD
Sgt. P A BURNELL-PHILLIPS
F/Lt. N W BURNETT
Sgt. O V BURNS
Sgt. A D BURT

Sgt. A A BURTENSHAW
F/Sgt. C G BURTON
S/Ldr. H F BURTON
P/O L G BURTON
Sgt. B M BUSH
Sgt. G D BUSHELL
Sgt. S L BUTTERFIELD
Sgt. A F BUTTERICK
AC2 K BUTTERWORTH
Sgt. E L BYRNE
Sgt. A R CAIN
P/O J R CAISTER
P/O G D CALDERHEAD
Sgt. T M CALDERWOOD
F/Lt. W P CAMBRIDGE
Sgt. J D CAMERON
F/Sgt. M CAMERON
Sgt. N CAMERON
F/Lt. A M CAMPBELL
Sgt. D C O CAMPBELL
P/O G L CAMPBELL
F/Lt. E W CAMPBELL-COLQUHOUN
P/O R J CANDY
Sgt. A W CANHAM
AC1 B CANNON
Sgt. B CAPEL
P/O C F A CAPON
P/O P M CARDELL
P/O C F CARDNELL
F/Lt. F R CAREY
P/O S CARLIN
F/O W F CARNABY
Sgt. R CARNALL
P/O J M V CARPENTER
F/Lt. W J CARR
Sgt. R A CARR-LEWTY
Sgt. L R CARTER
F/O P E G CARTER
P/O V A CARTER

F/O J C CARVER
P/O K M CARVER
Lt.(FAA) R H P CARVER
P/O H R CASE
F/O E CASSIDY
P/O L H CASSON
Sgt. C E P CASTLE
F/Lt. J G CAVE
P/O F N CAWSE
Sgt. D F CHADWICK
P/O R I CHAFFE
P/O H H CHALDER
W/Cdr. G P CHAMBERLAIN
P/O J T R CHAMBERLAIN
Sgt. H H CHANDLER
Sgt. V R CHAPMAN
P/O A K CHAPPELL
F/O C G CHAPPELL
Sgt. D W E CHAPPLE
Sgt. W T CHARD
AC2 G CHARNOCK
Sgt. H W CHARNOCK
Sgt. J C CHEETHAM
P/O P CHESTERS
P/O C A C CHETHAM
Sgt. C A CHEW
W/Cdr. R A CHIGNELL
Sub/Lt.(FAA) P C S CHILTON
Sgt. D J CHIPPING
F/O R A CHISHOLM
Sgt. J McB CHRISTIE
S/Ldr. W M CHURCHILL
F/Lt. D L CLACKSON
Sgt. J A CLANDILLON
S/Ldr. D De B CLARK
Sgt. G P CLARK
F/O H D CLARK
Sgt. W T CLARK
P/O A W CLARKE
Sgt. G S CLARKE

Sgt. G T CLARKE
Sgt. H R CLARKE
S/Ldr. R N CLARKE
F/O R W CLARKE
F/O G N S CLEAVER
Sgt. I C C CLENSHAW
F/Lt. R F H CLERKE
F/O D G CLIFT
P/O J K G CLIFTON
P/O A V CLOWES
F/Lt. W P CLYDE
Lt.(FAA) J P COATES
Lt.Cdr.(FAA) J C COCKBURN
Lt.(FAA) R C COCKBURN
P/O J COGGINS
F/Lt. J H COGHLAN
F/O D A COKE
Sgt. C F J COLE
P/O C COLEBROOK
P/O E J COLEMAN
F/O P COLLARD
Sgt. G R COLLETT
P/O L W COLLINGRIDGE
S/Ldr. A R COLLINS
P/O P W COMELY
F/Lt. H A G COMERFORD
AC2 J W COMPTON
F/O F H P CONNOR
F/Lt. S D P CONNORS
F/O M H CONSTABLE MAXWELL
Sgt. A W COOK
Sgt. H COOK
Sgt. R V COOK
F/Lt. C A COOKE
Sgt. H R COOKE
Sgt. E COOMBES
Sgt. R J COOMBS
F/Sgt. C J COONEY
S/Ldr. W E COOPE

AC2 C F COOPER	F/Lt. P A N COX	F/O M B CZERNIN	Sgt. F S DAY	W/Cdr. E M DONALDSON	Sgt. W L DYMOND
Sgt. D C COOPER	Sgt. R C R COX	P/O R C DAFFORN	F/O R L F DAY	Sgt. W S DOSSETT	Sgt. A W EADE
Sgt. J E COOPER	Sgt. W E COX	Sgt. P A DALE	Sgt. A H DEACON	F/O N A R DOUGHTY	Sgt. EARLEY
Sgt. R N COOPER	Sgt. J H COXON	Sgt. R W DALTON	P/O R DEACON-ELLIOTT	P/O W A DOUGLAS	Sgt. R L EARP
Sgt. S F COOPER	Sgt. D B CRABTREE	S/Ldr. T F DALTON-MORGAN	Sgt. H G DEADMAN	F/O M D DOULTON	Sgt. D A EASTON
Sgt. T A COOPER	F/Lt. G D CRAIG	Sgt. J J DALY	F/Lt. E C DEANESLY	P/O B DOUTHWAITE	F/O A F ECKFORD
P/O A M COOPER-KEY	Sgt. J T CRAIG	Sgt. J E DANN	P/O K B L DEBENHAM	F/O D H T DOWDING	F/Lt. A R EDGE
F/O T P M COOPER-SLIPPER	Sgt. E W CRANWELL	LAC A G DANNATT	Sgt. O J DEE	Sgt. J K DOWN	S/Ldr. G R EDGE
Sgt. L E M COOTE	Sgt. D G CRESSWELL	F/O B W J D'ARCY-IRVINE	Sgt. A L M DELLER	F/O P D McL DOWN	Sgt. A EDGLEY
Sgt. R COPCUTT	F/O E D CREW	Sgt. A McD S DARGIE	P/O R A DeMANCHA	AC1 T DRABY	P/O G A F EDMISTON
Sgt. N D COPELAND	Sgt. J L CRISP	W/Cdr. H S DARLEY	F/O R S DEMETRIADI	F/Lt. B DRAKE	F/O H P M EDRIDGE
Sgt. P COPELAND	P/O R F CROCKETT	Sgt. A S DARLING	P/O G A DENBY	P/O B V DRAPER	P/O E F EDSALL
P/O J H H COPEMAN	F/O P G CROFTS	Sgt. E V DARLING	Sgt. H D DENCHFIELD	P/O G G F DRAPER	Sgt. A J EDWARDS
Sgt. W J CORBIN	Sgt. R CROMBIE	P/O C W W DARWIN	S/Ldr. G L DENHOLM	Sgt. R A DRAPPER	Sgt. F EDWARDS
Sgt. H CORCORAN	P/O D M CROOK	P/O B DAVEY	Sgt. D A DENTON	Sgt. A S DREDGE	Sgt. H H EDWARDS
Sgt. H A CORDELL	Sgt. H K CROOK	P/O J A J DAVEY	P/O J M DERBYSHIRE	P/O N G DREVER	P/O I H EDWARDS
Sgt. D F CORFE	Sgt. M E CROSKELL	F/Lt. W D DAVID	Sgt. D C DEUNTZER	S/Ldr. P E DREW	P/O K C EDWARDS
Sub/Lt.(FAA) R J CORK	P/O J T CROSSEY	Sgt. H J DAVIDSON	S/Ldr. P K DEVITT	F/O J F DRUMMOND	Sgt. EDWARDS
P/O A H CORKETT	S/Ldr. M N CROSSLEY	P/O A E DAVIES	F/O J M F DEWAR	P/O J H DUART	Sgt. G H EDWORTHY
P/O N H CORRY	Sgt. R G CROSSMAN	P/O G G A DAVIES	W/Cdr. J S DEWAR	P.O.(FAA) R E DUBBER	S/Ldr. H EELES
F/O G W CORY	P/O H R CROWLEY	S/Ldr. J A DAVIES	P/O R B DEWEY	P/O B L DUCKENFIELD	Sgt. E J EGAN
Sgt. E T COSBY	P/O D CROWLEY-MILLING	Sgt. L DAVIES	P/O K S DEWHURST	P/O S S DUFF	Sgt. V H EKINS
P/O I H COSBY	P/O I J A CRUICKSHANKS	Sgt. M P DAVIES	F/O P G DEXTER	F/Lt. R M B D DUKE-	Sgt. D W ELCOME
P/O D V C COTES-PREEDY	P/O J CRUTTENDEN	F/O P F McD DAVIES	P/O R G E DIAMANT	WOOLLEY	Sgt. F W ELEY
AC2 G COTTAM	AC2 R W CULLEN	F/O R B DAVIES	P/O W G DICKIE	Sgt. W H DULWICH	P/O F R C ELGER
P/O H W COTTAM	Sgt. J D CULMER	F/O P J DAVIES-COOKE	Sgt. J H DICKINSON	Sgt. DUNCAN	P/O H W ELIOT
F/O R N H COURTNEY	Sgt. J H CULVERWELL	Sgt. A S DAVIS	Sgt. M P DIGBY-WORSLEY	F/O H S L DUNDAS	P/O J F D ELKINGTON
Sgt. H W COUSSENS	Sgt. A B CUMBERS	P/O C T DAVIS	Sgt. J W DITZEL	F/O J C DUNDAS	P/O J L W ELLACOMBE
P/O G W COUZENS	Sgt. J CUNNINGHAM	Sgt. J DAVIS	Sgt. C A W DIXON	Sgt. J T DUNMORE	P/O C C ELLERY
F/O W H COVERLEY	F/Lt. J CUNNINGHAM	Sgt. J N DAVIS	Sgt. F J P DIXON	Sgt. I L DUNN	P/O G E ELLIS
P/O A R COVINGTON	F/Lt. J L G CUNNINGHAM	Sgt. P E DAVIS	Sgt. G DIXON	P/O P W DUNNING-WHITE	S/Ldr. J ELLIS
F/Lt. J B COWARD	P/O W CUNNINGHAM	Sgt. P O DAVIS	F/O J A DIXON	Sgt. R D DUNSCOMBE	Sgt. J H M ELLIS
AC2 W COWEN	Sgt. W G CUNNINGTON	Sgt. W L DAVIS	LAC L DIXON	S/Ldr. F P R DUNWORTH	Sgt. R V ELLIS
Sgt. J COWLEY	Sgt. T CUPITT	F/O T D H DAVY	F/O N R DOBREE	Sgt. O A DUPEE	Sgt. W T ELLIS
Sgt. J R COWSILL	P/O J CURCHIN	F/O V G DAW	P/O J D DODD	LAC G W DUTTON	Sgt. H D B ELSDON
Sgt. D G S R COX	Sgt. A G CURLEY	P/O P L DAWBARN	Sgt. C W DODGE	F/Lt. R G DUTTON	F/Lt. T A F ELSDON
F/O G J COX	F/Lt. C F CURRANT	Sgt. T DAWSON	P/O R F T DOE	P/O R A L DUVIVER	Sgt. P ELSE
Sgt. G P COX	Sgt. F W CURTIS	Sub/Lt.(FAA) F DAWSON-	P/O R S DON	Sgt. B E DYE	Sgt. G EMMETT
P/O K H COX	F/O J W CUTTS	PAUL	F/Lt. I D G DONALD	Sgt. L A DYKE	F/Lt. W A C EMMETT

P/O C E ENGLISH
F/O P S B ENSOR
Sgt. W J ETHERINGTON
Sgt. C R EVANS
P/O D EVANS
Sgt. G J EVANS
P/O H A C EVANS
Sgt. W R EVANS
Sgt. A D EVERETT
Sgt. G C EVERITT
Sgt. P R EYLES
F/O A EYRE
F/Lt. W R FARLEY
F/Lt. J N W FARMER
P/O E FARNES
Sgt. P C P FARNES
W/Cdr. A D FARQUHAR
Sgt. J R FARROW
Sgt. J FARTHING
Sgt. D P FAWCETT
Sgt. A N FEARY
Sgt. J L FEATHER
Sgt. S A FENEMORE
Sgt. C F FENN
S/Ldr. H A FENTON
P/O J O FENTON
P/O C R FENWICK
P/O R F FERDINAND
Sgt. E H FERGUSON
F/Lt. P J FERGUSON
F/Lt. H M FERRISS
AC F FILDES
S/Ldr. D O FINLAY
P/O A FINNIE
F/Lt. J F F FINNIS
F/O A G A FISHER
F/O B M FISHER
F/O G FISHER
Sgt. J F FIZEL

P/O R D S FLEMING
Sgt. J D FLETCHER
Sgt. J G B FLETCHER
P/O J FLINDERS
Sgt. H L FLOWER
Sgt. R H FOKES
AC J H FOLLIARD
S/Ldr. A S FORBES
Sgt. R C FORD
F/O D N FORDE
Sgt. D H FORREST
P/O G M FORRESTER
F/Lt. T H T FORSHAW
F/O A D FORSTER
Sgt. R V FORWARD
P/O R W FOSTER
Sgt. A C FOTHERINGHAM
Sgt. R J FOWLER
Sgt. L FOX
Sgt. P H FOX
F/O C N FOXLEY-NORRIS
P/O D H FOX-MALE
P/O C D FRANCIS
Sgt. C W FRANCIS
Sgt. D N FRANCIS
Sgt. J FRANCIS
F/O N I C FRANCIS
F/O W D K FRANKLIN
P/O W H FRANKLIN
Sgt. R H B FRASER
F/Lt. J C FREEBORN
Sgt. R P FREEMAN
Sgt. P F FREER
Sgt. L E FREESE
Sgt. T L FRENCH
Sgt. J R FRIEND
P/O A H B FRIENDSHIP
Sgt. J H FRIPP
F/O E M FRISBY

Sgt. E T G FRITH
P/O J L FROST
Sgt. D FULFORD
Sgt. R H FURNEAUX
P/O D H GAGE
F/O D R GAMBLEN
P/O S R GANE
Sgt. E GANT
Sgt. E C GARDINER
F/O F T GARDINER
Sgt. W N GARDINER
Sgt. B G D GARDNER
F/Lt. P M GARDNER
Sub/Lt.(FAA) R E GARDNER
Sgt. W J GARFIELD
P/O A H H GARRAD
Sgt. G GARSIDE
Sgt. G W GARTON
Sgt. L A GARVEY
S/Ldr. G D GARVIN
Sgt. F GASH
P/O R S GASKELL
P/O G N GAUNT
Sgt. W E GAUNT
Sgt. A GAVAN
F/Lt. J R H GAYNER
Sgt. A W GEAR
F/O K I GEDDES
Sgt. V D GEE
P/O T GENNEY
Sgt. R J K GENT
Sgt. R P FREEMAN
Sgt. D G GIBBINS
Sgt. C M GIBBONS
F/Lt. H S GIDDINGS
P/O E G GILBERT
F/O H T GILBERT
Mid.(FAA) P R J GILBERT
Sgt. J S GILDERS
Sgt. J V GILL

F/Lt. D E GILLAM
Sgt. E GILLAM
F/O J GILLAN
F/O T W GILLEN
P/O J L GILLESPIE
Sgt. J GILLIES
F/Lt. K McL GILLIES
P/O K R GILLMAN
F/O G K GILROY
Sgt. H R GILYEAT
Sgt. A G GIRDWOOD
P/O E D GLASER
S/Ldr. T P GLEAVE
Sgt. G GLEDHILL
F/Lt. I R GLEED
P/O A J GLEGG
Sgt. J N GLENDINNING
Sgt. N V GLEW
F/Lt. H G GODDARD
F/Lt. W B GODDARD
W/Cdr. S F GODDEN
Sgt. J E GOLDSMITH
P/O H I GOODALL
Sgt. A T GOODERHAM
Sgt. G GOODMAN
P/O G E GOODMAN
Sgt. M V GOODMAN
Sgt. C GOODWIN
F/O H McD GOODWIN
Sgt. R D GOODWIN
Sgt. S A GOODWIN
P/O R L GOORD
Sgt. S GORDON
P/O W H G GORDON
F/Lt. W E GORE
P/O D G GORRIE
P/O R C GOSLING
Sgt. E C GOTHORPE
F/O D L GOULD

F/Sgt. G L GOULD
Sgt. R J GOULDSTONE
P/O G K GOUT
F/O A V GOWERS
F/Lt. E J GRACIE
S/Ldr. E GRAHAM
Sgt. J GRAHAM
P/O K A G GRAHAM
S/Ldr. J GRANDY
Sub/Lt.(FAA) D GRANT
Sgt. E J F GRANT
F/O S B GRANT
Sgt. E A GRAVES
P/O R C GRAVES
F/O A P GRAY
P/O C K GRAY
P/O D McI GRAY
Sgt. K W GRAY
Sgt. M GRAY
P/O T GRAY
F/Sgt. C GRAYSON
P/O A W V GREEN
F/Lt. C P GREEN
Sgt. F W W GREEN
Sgt. G G GREEN
Sgt. H E GREEN
P/O M D GREEN
Sgt. W J GREEN
Sub/Lt.(FAA) H laF
    GREENSHIELDS
P/O J P B GREENWOOD
Sgt. A E GREGORY
Sgt. A H GREGORY
P/O F S GREGORY
Sgt. W J GREGORY
P/O H E GRELLIS
Sgt. K G GRESTY
Sgt. R H GRETTON
F/Lt. D G GRIBBLE

F/O D H GRICE
F/O D N GRICE
Sgt. R V GRIDLEY
F/O T GRIER
Sgt. J J GRIFFIN
Sgt. C G GRIFFITH
Sgt. G GRIFFITHS
Sgt. H C GROVE
Sgt. E G GRUBB
Sgt. H F GRUBB
P/O T F GUEST
P/O K C GUNDRY
P/O H R GUNN
P/O P S GUNNING
P/O E M GUNTER
P/O J V GURTEEN
Lt.(FAA) G C McE GUTHRIE
Sgt. N H GUTHRIE
Sgt. L N GUY
Mid.(FAA) P GUY
Sgt. E N L GUYMER
P/O G H HACKWOOD
F/Lt. J G E HAIG
Sgt. C HAIGH
P/O R C HAINE
F/O L A HAINES
Sgt. J K HAIRE
P/O P R HAIRS
Sgt. R HALL
F/Lt. N M HALL
Sgt. P F HALL
P/O R C HALL
P/O R M D HALL
P/O W C HALL
F/Lt. I L McG HALLAM
F/O A B HALLIWELL
Sgt. H J L HALLOWES
Sgt. D W HALTON
P/O J R HAMAR

W/Cdr. R K HAMBLIN	Sgt. C HAW	P/O A H HILES	P/O D F HOLLAND	P/O P HOWES	F/Lt. A INGLE
Sgt. R C HAMER	Sgt. P S HAWKE	Sgt. C G HILKEN	F/Lt. R H HOLLAND	P/O G L HOWITT	P/O M R INGLE-FINCH
P/O A C HAMILTON	Sgt. S N HAWKE	P/O A E HILL	Sgt. R M HOLLAND	Sgt. I E HOWITT	Sgt. R A INNES
Sgt. C B HAMILTON	Sgt. R P HAWKINGS	Sgt. A M HILL	Sgt. E J HOLLIS	Sgt. G V HOYLE	F/O R F INNESS
P/O C E HAMILTON	Sgt. F B HAWLEY	Sgt. C R HILL	Sgt. S V HOLLOWAY	Sgt. H N HOYLE	F/Lt. M M IRVING
Sgt. J S HAMILTON	F/O J F J HAWORTH	Sgt. G HILL	Sgt. K B HOLLOWELL	Sgt. B F R HUBBARD	Sgt. L R ISAAC
Sgt. R F HAMLYN	Lt.(FAA) R C HAY	P/O G E HILL	Sgt. E L HOLMES	F/Lt. T E HUBBARD	Sgt. D W ISHERWOOD
Sgt. J HAMMERTON	Sgt. L H HAYDEN	S/Ldr. J H HILL	P/O F H HOLMES	Sgt. P E HUCKIN	Sgt. T C IVESON
P/O D J HAMMOND	S/Ldr. H L HAYES	P/O S J HILL	P/O G H HOLMES	Sgt. A J HUGHES	Sgt. R IVEY
Sgt. C E HAMPSHIRE	F/Lt. T N HAYES	F/O R H HILLARY	Sgt. R T HOLMES	F/Lt. D P HUGHES	F/Lt. D MacF JACK
P/O O V HANBURY	Sgt. R A HAYLOCK	F/Lt. H B L HILLCOAT	Sgt. W B HOLROYD	P/O D L HUGHES	AC2 A JACKSON
F/O E L HANCOCK	Sgt. D HAYWOOD	Sgt. R W HILLMAN	Sgt. A G V HOLTON	F/O F D HUGHES	Sgt. P F JACKSON
P/O N E HANCOCK	Sgt. F A P HEAD	Sgt. P HILLWOOD	F/O M G HOMER	F/Lt. J McC M HUGHES	P/O H JACOBS
P/O N P W HANCOCK	P/O G M HEAD	Sgt. M H HINE	P/O D H HONE	Sgt. W R K HUGHES	AC1 N JACOBSON
P/O G H HANNAN	F/Lt. P W D HEAL	Sgt. L HIRD	F/O D S G HONOR	Sgt. J A HUGHES-REES	AC1 R H JAMES
F/O D H W HANSON	Sgt. T W R HEALY	F/O B A H HITCHINGS	S/Ldr. H R L HOOD	Sgt. D J HULBERT	Sgt. R S S JAMES
F/O J R HARDACRE	F/Lt. B HEATH	Sgt. A J B HITHERSAY	Sgt. A HOOK	Sgt. F H R HULBERT	Sgt. R W E JARRETT
Sgt. J HARDCASTLE	P/O G S HEBRON	P/O J H HOARE-SCOTT	P/O D N HOOKWAY	F/Lt. J B W HUMPHERSON	P/O D T JAY
Sgt. G HARDIE	P/O A L HEDGES	P/O D O HOBBIS	F/O B G HOOPER	P/O A H HUMPHREY	F/O M JEBB
F/Lt. N M HARDING	Sgt. D A HELCKE	P/O J B HOBBS	S/Ldr. A P HOPE	F/O J D HUMPHREYS	F/Lt. R V JEFF
Sgt. N D HARDING	F/Lt. R O HELLYER	Sgt. S J HOBBS	F/O R HOPE	P/O P C HUMPHREYS	P/O H J JEFFCOAT
Sgt. W R H HARDWICK	F/O J A M HENDERSON	P/O C A HOBSON	Sgt. J HOPEWELL	P/O P H HUMPHREYS	F/Lt. J JEFFERIES
Sgt. O A HARDY	AC1 D O HENDRY	F/Lt. D B HOBSON	Sgt. C L HOPGOOD	Sgt. D A C HUNT	Sgt. G JEFFERSON
P/O R HARDY	Sgt. W B HENN	S/Ldr. W F C HOBSON	P/O W P HOPKIN	P/O D W HUNT	P/O S F JEFFERSON
Sgt. M T HARE	Sgt. B HENSON	AC1 W H HODDS	Sgt. B W HOPTON	P/O H N HUNT	Sgt. H R JEFFERY-CRIDGE
P/O F N HARGREAVES	F/Lt. L F HENSTOCK	Sgt. J S A HODGE	Sgt. W H HORNBY	F/Lt. A S HUNTER	Sgt. G W JEFFERYS
Sgt. A S HARKER	P/O H M T HERON	Sgt. A J HODGKINSON	Sgt. F G HORNER	Sgt. D J HUNTER	F/O A J O JEFFREY
F/Lt. W J HARPER	Sgt. V W HESLOP	S/Ldr. H A V HOGAN	P/O J M HORROX	S/Ldr. P A HUNTER	P/O C G St.D JEFFRIES
P/O P A HARRIS	Sgt. E L HETHERINGTON	P/O D W HOGG	P/O H B L HOUGH	F/Lt. J H HUNTER-TOD	P/O D N O JENKINS
Sgt. A R J HARRISON	Sgt. G A HEWETT	F/Lt. E S HOGG	P/O C G HOUGHTON	Sgt. C A L HURRY	Sgt. B J JENNINGS
P/O D S HARRISON	Sgt. C R HEWLETT	Sgt. J H HOGG	Sgt. O V HOUGHTON	P/O P R S HURST	Sub/Lt.(FAA) D M JERAM
P/O J H HARRISON	F/Lt. J M HEWSON	Sgt. R D HOGG	P/O J HOWARD	Sgt. I HUTCHINSON	Sgt. E R JESSOP
P/O F C HARROLD	S/Ldr. G F W HEYCOCK	P/O R M HOGG	P/O P I HOWARD-WILLIAMS	Sub/Lt.(FAA) D A HUTCHISON	Sgt. G B JOHNS
P/O K G HART	P/O N B HEYWOOD	Sgt. R V HOGG	Sgt. E F HOWARTH		Sgt. A E JOHNSON
F/O P McD HARTAS	S/Ldr. J H HEYWORTH	F/Lt. E HOLDEN	F/O B HOWE	P/O R R HUTLEY	P/O A E JOHNSON
Sgt. L W HARVEY	Sgt. D T HICK	F/O K HOLDEN	P/O D C HOWE	Sgt. R S HUTTON	Sgt. C A JOHNSON
P/O D HASTINGS	Sgt. W B HIGGINS	P/O G A HOLDER	F/Lt. F J HOWELL	Sgt. J W HYDE	P/O C E JOHNSON
Sgt. HATTON	P/O F W HIGGINSON	Sgt. R HOLDER	Sgt. F V HOWELL	F/O C P IGGLESDEN	P/O J E JOHNSON
Sgt. R E HAVERCROFT	F/O T P K HIGGS	S/Ldr. A L HOLLAND	Sgt. H N HOWES	Sgt. H S IMRAY	Sgt. J I JOHNSON

Sgt. R A JOHNSON	Sgt. W H KELLITT	Sgt. L A KOMAROFF	S/Ldr. J A LEATHART	Sgt. A J LIPSCOMBE	AC1 J LYNCH
Sgt. R B JOHNSON	F/Lt. R A KELLOW	P/O M KRAMER	P/O E G C LEATHEM	S/Ldr. R C F LISTER	P/O E B LYONS
Sgt. R K H JOHNSON	F/O L G H KELLS	Sgt. E R LACEY	F/Lt. W J LEATHER	P/O P LITCHFIELD	F/Lt. M R MACARTHUR
P/O S F F JOHNSON	S/Ldr. D P D G KELLY	Sgt. J H LACEY	Sgt. J Le CHEMINANT	Sgt. F W R LITSON	Sgt. A S MacDONALD
Sgt. W J JOHNSON	Sgt. E N KELSEY	Sgt. W L LACKIE	P/O J G LECKY	P/O A G LITTLE	P/O D K MACDONALD
S/Ldr. A V R JOHNSTONE	F/O J L KEMP	F/Lt. A J A LAING	Sgt. E F Le CONTE	F/Lt. B W LITTLE	S/Ldr. D S MacDONALD
P/O I K S JOLL	P/O N L D KEMP	P/O D M LAKE	Sgt. L LEDGER	S/Ldr. J H LITTLE	F/Lt. H K MacDONALD
F/Lt. C A T JONES	P/O J B KENDAL	AC1 A LAMB	Sgt. T LE DONG	Sgt. R LITTLE	S/Ldr. A R D MacDONELL
F/Lt. D A E JONES	F/Lt. H C KENNARD	F/Lt. P G LAMB	F/O K N T LEE	F/O A J A LLEWELLIN	Sgt. C W MACDOUGAL
Sgt. E JONES	P/O P F KENNARD-DAVIS	P/O R L LAMB	Sgt. M A W LEE	Sgt. R T LLEWELLYN	F/O I N MacDOUGALL
Sgt. H D B JONES	Sgt. R W KENNEDY	Sub/Lt.(FAA) R R LAMB	F/Lt. R H A LEE	AC LLOYD	S/Ldr. R I G MacDOUGALL
Sgt. J F R JONES	P/O P L KENNER	F/Lt. H M S LAMBERT	S/Ldr. R B LEES	Sgt. D E LLOYD	F/Lt. C H MACFIE
P/O J S B JONES	P/O P KENNETT	P/O W G M LAMBIE	P/O A F Y LEES	P/O J P LLOYD	Sgt. A N MacGREGOR
P/O J T JONES	Sgt. G KENSALL	P/O A LAMMER	F/O P W LEFEVRE	Sgt. P D LLOYD	Sgt. W H MACHIN
Sgt. K H JONES	P/O R D KENT	P/O L N LANDELS	P/O B P LEGGE	P/O E S LOCK	P/O R MacKAY
P/O R E JONES	F/Lt. R G KER-RAMSAY	Sgt. J LANSDELL	P/O P G LEGGETT	F/O J LOCKHART	P/O K W MACKENZIE
P/O R L JONES	P/O A KERSHAW	S/Ldr. B J E LANE	Sgt. A C LEIGH	Sgt. E E LOCKTON	Lt.(FAA) A McL
P/O W R JONES	Sub/Lt.(FAA) I H KESTIN	F/O R LANE	S/Ldr. R H A LEIGH	Sgt. J C LOCKWOOD	MACKINNON
P/O C C O JOUBERT	Sgt. M KEYMER	P/O N C LANGHAM-	P/O J D LENAHAN	F/O K T LOFTS	Sgt. D D MacKINNON
Sgt. L JOWITT	Sgt. J D KEYNES	HOBART	Sgt. M E LENG	P/O C LOGAN	S/Ldr. A M MACLACHLAN
P/O J R JULEFF	Sgt. P KILLICK	P/O G A LANGLEY	Mid.(FAA) P L LENNARD	P/O O A LOGIE	F/Lt. J A F MacLACHLAN
P/O A H E KAHN	Sgt. F W G KILLINGBACK	Sgt. L LANGLEY	F/O E C LENTON	P/O J LONSDALE	P/O A C MACLAREN
F/O T M KANE	P/O D S KINDER	P/O F C A LANNING	F/Lt. S P Le ROUGETEL	F/O D J LOOKER	F/Lt. C H MacLEAN
Sgt. L R KARASEK	Lt.(FAA) A T J KINDERSLEY	P/O B D LARBALESTIER	Sgt. F T LERWAY	F/Lt. M J LOUDON	Sgt. G S M MacLEOD
Sgt. A KAY	S/Ldr. E B KING	Sgt. A J LAUDER	Sgt. E W LESK	F/Lt. A D J LOVELL	F/O B R MACNAMARA
P/O D H S KAY	P/O F H KING	F/O J H LAUGHLIN	Sgt. G M LESLIE	Sgt. J E LOVERSEED	Sgt. A R D MACONOCHIE
P/O J K KAY	P/O L F D KING	Sgt. G LAURENCE	Sgt. S A LEVENSON	F/Lt. R E LOVETT	P/O J F J MACPHAIL
S/Ldr. J R KAYLL	P/O M A KING	Sgt. D N LAWFORD	Sgt. C S LEWIS	Sgt. J LOWE	F/Sgt. R R MACPHERSON
P/O J A KEARD	F/O P J C KING	Sgt. E S LAWLER	LAC J H LEWIS	P/O P A LOWETH	Sgt. I N MacRAE
Sgt. A W KEARSEY	P/O W L KING	Sgt. J T LAWRENCE	Sgt. W G LEWIS	AC1 W LOWTHER	Sgt. H I MacRORY
P/O P J KEARSEY	Sgt. D E KINGABY	Sgt. N A LAWRENCE	Sgt. R H LEYLAND	S/Ldr. W W LOXTON	P/O S J MADLE
Sgt. F J KEAST	F/Lt. C B F KINGCOME	P/O A F LAWS	Sgt. R LILLEY	P/O R M McT D LUCAS	P/O G H MAFFETT
Sgt. J KEATINGS	P/O R A KINGS	Sgt. G G S LAWS	Sgt. P LILLE	Sgt. S E LUCAS	P/O M H MAGGS
Sgt. E H C KEE	Sgt. T B KIRK	P/O R C LAWSON	Sgt. E R LIMPENNY	P/O D T M LUMSDEN	S/Ldr. H J MAGUIRE
Sgt. G E KEEL	F/Lt. M T KIRKWOOD	F/Lt. W J LAWSON	P/O A I LINDSAY	Sgt. J C LUMSDEN	P.O.(FAA) T J MAHONEY
Sgt. R R G KEELER	Sgt. D I KIRTON	P/O J LAWSON-BROWN	P/O P C LINDSEY	P/O J W LUND	Sgt. A D W MAIN
F/O G KEIGHLEY	P/O T R KITSON	F/Lt. P C F LAWTON	F/O A P LINES	Sgt. K R LUSTY	Sgt. H R MAIN
P/O M KELLETT	F/Lt. R A L KNIGHT	F/O H K LAYCOCK	P/O J G LINGARD	P/O A LYALL	P/O B MAITLAND-
S/Ldr. R G KELLETT	F/O W R A KNOCKER	P/O D C LEARY	F/O A S LINNEY	F/Lt. A McL LYALL	THOMPSON

F/Lt. W H MAITLAND-WALKER
Sgt. A E MAKINS
P/O E E MALES
Sgt. R S MALLETT
P/O K MANGER
P/O H J MANN
Sgt. J MANN
P/O J MANSEL-LEWIS
Sgt. B M MANSFIELD
Sgt. D E MANSFIELD
Sgt. E MANTON
S/Ldr. G A L MANTON
P/O R A MARCHAND
Sgt. R G MARLAND
F/O R MARPLES
P/O E S MARRS
Lt.(FAA) A E MARSH
Sgt. E H MARSH
Sgt. H J MARSH
Sgt. W C MARSH
Sgt. A E MARSHALL
F/Lt. J E MARSHALL
P/O J V MARSHALL
Sgt. T B MARSHALL
Sgt. T R MARSHALL
P/O G MARSLAND
P/O K J MARSTON
Sgt. A MARTIN
P/O A W MARTIN
Sub/Lt.(FAA) R M S MARTIN
Sgt. T A MASLEN
Sgt. W MASON
Sgt. K MASSEY
P/O J R MATHER
Sgt. J W MATHERS
F/Lt. G C MATHESON
P/O K MATHEWS
Sgt. H G MATTHEWS

F/O H K F MATTHEWS
Sgt. I W MATTHEWS
F/O P G H MATTHEWS
P/O D A MAXWELL
S/Ldr. H L MAXWELL
Sgt. W MAXWELL
F/O P F MAYHEW
W/O E MAYNE
Sgt. J McADAM
Sgt. W D McADAM
Sgt. P J McALISTER
F/Lt. J H G McARTHUR
Sgt. T A McCANN
Sgt. J P McCARTHY
Sgt. T F McCARTHY
AC2 J P McCAUL
F/O D C McCAW
P/O J A P McCLINTOCK
S/Ldr. J E McCOMB
Sgt. J McCONNELL
Sgt. J B McCORMACK
P/O R McDOUGALL
Sgt. A McDOWALL
P/O A McFADDEN
P/O J McGIBBON
P/O K B McGLASHAN
F/O R A McGOWAN
P/O R H McGOWAN
P/O J K U B McGRATH
P/O A J McGREGOR
F/O P R McGREGOR
Sgt. R McGUGAN
F/O D B H McHARDY
P/O A McINNES
Sgt. P R C McINTOSH
Sgt. D A S McKAY
S/Ldr. A A McKELLAR
P/O J W McKENZIE
Sgt. E J McKIE

Sgt. J W McLAUGHLIN
P/O A C R McLURE
Sgt. J R McMAHON
F/O D A P McMULLEN
Sgt. R J McNAIR
Sgt. A L McNAY
Sgt. J McPHEE
P/O J R B MEAKER
S/Ldr. S T MEARES
F/Lt. W E G MEASURES
Sgt. J C O MEDWORTH
Sgt. C V MEESON
F/O J C MELVILL
P/O G H MELVILLE-JACKSON
Sgt. T N MENAGE
Sgt. R T D MERCER
Sgt. H J MERCHANT
Sgt. A D MEREDITH
W/Cdr. H W MERMAGEN
Sgt. J C MERRETT
P/O C MERRICK
Sgt. S W MERRYWEATHER
Sgt. B W MESNER
Sgt. A C METCALFE
Sgt. J METHAM
Sgt. R H R MEYER
Sgt. W MIDDLEMISS
Sgt. R A MILBURN
P/O P R MILDREN
P/O D E MILEHAM
Sgt. E E MILES
Sgt. S F MILES
F/O M J MILEY
P/O J G P MILLARD
Sgt. A C MILLER
AC1 A J MILLER
S/Ldr. A G MILLER
F/Lt. R MILLER

P/O R F G MILLER
AC T H MILLER
P/O K M MILLIST
AC1 J B MILLS
Sgt. J P MILLS
S/Ldr. R S MILLS
F/O R M MILNE
Sgt. A H MILNES
Sgt. G MITCHELL
P/O G T M MITCHELL
S/Ldr. H M MITCHELL
F/O L R G MITCHELL
Sgt. D C MITCHELL
P/O P H G MITCHELL
Sgt. R R MITCHELL
F/O G E MOBERLY
Sgt. D A MONK
P/O E W J MONK
S/Ldr. G W MONTAGU
F/Lt. A MONTAGU-SMITH
P/O C R MONTGOMERY
Sgt. H F MONTGOMERY
Sgt. D G MOODY
P/O H W MOODY
Sgt. A R MOORE
P/O W R MOORE
W/Cdr. J W C MORE
F/Lt. R E G MOREWOOD
F/Sgt. P F MORFILL
P/O P J MORGAN
F/O H MORGAN-GRAY
P/O G E MORRIS
P/O J MORRIS
Sgt. J P MORRISON
Sgt. N MORRISON
F/O O B MORROGH-RYAN
P/O P A MORTIMER
F/O J S MORTON
Sgt. R C MOSS

Sub/Lt.(FAA) W J M MOSS
Sgt. W H MOTT
P/O R MOTTRAM
Sgt. E A MOULD
Sgt. E W MOULTON
P/O M H MOUNSDON
F/Lt. C J MOUNT
Sgt. R I MOWAT
Sgt. H F J MOYNHAM
P/O M R MUDIE
F/Lt. I J MUIRHEAD
F/Lt. J C MUNGO-PARK
F/Sgt. W S MUNN
S/Ldr. J G MUNRO
P/O L C MURCH
S/Ldr. A D MURRAY
Sgt. J MURRAY
Sgt. P H MURRAY
P/O T B MURRAY
Sgt. K E NAISH
Sgt. H T NAUGHTIN
P/O T F NEIL
F/Sgt. D NELSON
F/O G H NELSON-EDWARDS
Sgt. W J NEVILLE
F/O J C NEWBERY
Sgt. E A NEWHAM
F/O M A NEWLING
Sgt. D V NEWPORT
Sgt. E F NEWTON
Sgt. H S NEWTON
F/O J B H NICHOLAS
Sgt. D B F NICHOLLS
Sgt. T G F NICHOLLS
Sgt. D H NICHOLS
F/Lt. J B NICOLSON
Sgt. P B NICOLSON
P/O F G NIGHTINGALE
Sgt. W NIXON

P/O B R NOBLE
Sgt. D NOBLE
Sgt. W J NOBLE
F/O B NOKES-COOPER
P/O N R NORFOLK
Sgt. P P NORRIS
F/Lt. S C NORRIS
P/O G NORTH
Sgt. D J NORTH-BOMFORD
Sgt. J K NORWELL
P/O R K C NORWOOD
Sub/Lt.(FAA) W R NOWELL
P/O S G NUNN
Sgt. R R J NUTE
Sgt. R C NUTTER
S/Ldr. J S O'BRIEN
Sgt. P O'BYRNE
P/O A O'CONNELL
S/Ldr. N C ODBERT
P/O D B OGILVIE
Sgt. T G OLDFIELD
Sgt. A A O'LEARY
P/O W P OLESEN
Sgt. G D OLIVER
P/O P OLVER
F/O D K C O'MALLEY
F/O J J O'MEARA
Sgt. R J OMMANNEY
F/O D H O'NEILL
F/Lt. J A O'NEILL
Sgt. H C ORCHARD
P/O A G OSMAND
F/O C N OVERTON
Sgt. A E OWEN
Sgt. H OWEN
Sgt. W G OWEN
F/Lt. R W OXSPRING
Sgt. A D PAGE
F/O A G PAGE

Sgt. A J PAGE
F/Lt. C L PAGE
Sgt. V D PAGE
Sgt. W T PAGE
P/O F G PAISEY
Sgt. G C C PALLISER
Sgt. N N PALMER
Sub/Lt.(FAA) T R V PARKE
Sgt. D K PARKER
W/Cdr. I R PARKER
Sgt. K B PARKER
F/O T C PARKER
Sgt. W B PARKES
P/O E G PARKIN
Sgt. C PARKINSON
F/Lt. D G PARNALL
P/O S B PARNALL
Sgt. D J PARR
Sgt. L A PARR
F/O D T PARROTT
F/O P L PARROTT
Sgt. R J PARROTT
AC2 E PARRY
Sgt. M E PARRY
Sgt. C A PARSONS
Sgt. J G PARSONS
F/O P T PARSONS
F/O C W PASSY
Lt.(FAA) B PATERSON
Sgt. L F PATRICK
LAC A G PATSTON
F/Lt. H P F PATTEN
Sgt. L J PATTERSON
Sub/Lt.(FAA) N H
  PATTERSON
Mid.(FAA) P J PATTERSON
P/O R L PATTERSON
F/O A J S PATTINSON
Sgt. K C PATTISON

P/O W B PATTULLO
Sgt. H J PAVITT
Sgt. A D PAYNE
P/O R A PAYNE
AC2 R I PAYNE
P/O A J M PEACE
P/O C B G PEACHMENT
Sgt. D C PEACOCK
F/O R J PEACOCK
Sgt. W A PEACOCK
Sgt. L H B PEARCE
Sgt. P G PEARCE
Sgt. R PEARCE
Sgt. W J PEARCE
Sgt. D J PEARCY
P/O S J PEARMAIN
Sgt. L L PEARSE
Sgt. D E PEARSON
Sgt. G W PEARSON
Sgt. P PEARSON
F/O A P PEASE
Sgt. W PEEBLES
F/O C D PEEL
S/Ldr. J R A PEEL
F/O C O J PEGGE
S/Ldr. D A PEMBERTON
P/O P E PENFOLD
Sgt. W D PENFOLD
F/Sgt. V W R PENFORD
P/O D A PENNINGTON
F/Lt. A W PENNINGTON-
  LEGH
Sgt. B PENNYCUICK
F/O H H PERCY
Sgt. F S PERKIN
Sgt. H T PERRY
F/O G C B PETERS
P/O A H PETTET
Sgt. H W PETTIT

F/Lt. R D PEXTON
Sgt. J PHILLIP
Sgt. A PHILLIPS
P/O E R PHILLIPS
F/Sgt. N T PHILLIPS
Sgt. R F P PHILLIPS
AC1 J R PHILLIPSON
P/O R F PHILO
Sgt. J PICKERING
P/O J H PICKERING
Sgt. T G PICKERING
Sgt. J T PICKFORD
Sgt. L PIDD
F/O O St.J PIGG
Sgt. A PILKINGTON
F/O D J C PINCKNEY
S/Ldr. H M PINFOLD
S/Ldr. P C PINKHAM
Sgt. A H PIPER
P/O H A PIPPARD
P/O J G PIPPET
F/O G E PITTMAN
Sgt. R E PLANT
P/O G F C PLEDGER
Sgt. R PLENDERLEITH
F/O R P PLUMMER
Sgt. M H POCOCK
Sgt. J K POLLARD
F/O P S C POLLARD
F/Sgt. A H D POND
P/O W A PONTING
P/O P D POOL
Sgt. E L R POOLE
Sgt. E F PORTER
Sgt. J A PORTER
Sgt. J A POTTER
P/O H R G POULTON
Sgt. R R C POUND
Sgt. E POWELL

F/Lt. R P R POWELL
P/O R J POWELL
Sgt. S W M POWELL
F/Lt. G S ff POWELL-
  SHEDDEN
Sgt. S G PREATER
P/O A O PRICE
Sgt. J PRICE
Sgt. N A J PRICE
Sgt. R B PRICE
Sgt. J PROCTOR
F/Lt. J E PROCTOR
Sgt. P R PROSSER
Sgt. D H PROUDMAN
P/O H A R PROWSE
Sub/Lt.(FAA) G B PUDNEY
Sgt. J S PUGH
F/Lt. T P PUGH
F/Lt. A R PUTT
Sgt. W G V PUXLEY
F/O L L PYMAN
Sgt. B H QUELCH
F/O J K QUILL
Sgt. J QUINN
F/Lt. A C RABAGLIATI
F/Lt. J H M RABONE
P/O W P H RAFTER
Sgt. W RAINE
Sgt. D N RAINS
Sgt. L F RALLS
P/O J B RAMSAY
Sgt. J S RAMSAY
Sgt. N H D RAMSAY
Sgt. J W RAMSHAW
P/O H C RANDALL
F/O M RAVENHILL
F/O A J RAWLENCE
Sgt. C F RAWNSLEY
Sgt. R W RAY

F/O R M S RAYNER
P/O W A A READ
Sgt. C A REAM
Sub/Lt.(FAA) J REARDON-
  PARKER
Sgt. L A E REDDINGTON
Sgt. E A REDFERN
P/O J REDMAN
Sgt. L H M REECE
AC1 W E REECE
Sgt. H REED
F/O B V REES
P/O R REID
Sgt. J V RENVOIZE
P/O R A RHODES
F/Lt. W H RHODES-
  MOORHOUSE
F/O A L RICALTON
Sgt. P G RICH
Sub/Lt.(FAA) D H RICHARDS
Sgt. W C RICHARDS
Sgt. E RICHARDSON
Sgt. R W RICHARDSON
Sgt. R W RICHARDSON
S/Ldr. W A RICHARDSON
Sgt. H W RICKETTS
P/O V A RICKETTS
Sgt. J D RIDDELL-HANNAM
F/Lt. C J H RIDDLE
F/Lt. H J RIDDLE
Sgt. M RIDLEY
P/O R H RIGBY
P/O F RILEY
F/Lt. W RILEY
F/Lt. R F RIMMER
Sgt. E A RINGWOOD
Sgt. W G RIPLEY
P/O A J RIPPON
Sgt. A H RISELEY

F/O G L RITCHER
F/Lt. I S RITCHIE
P/O J M RITCHIE
P/O J R RITCHIE
Sgt. R D RITCHIE
P/O T G F RITCHIE
P/O R J B ROACH
P/O R A L ROBB
Sgt. R H ROBBINS
Sgt. A J A ROBERTS
Sgt. D F ROBERTS
W/Cdr. D N ROBERTS
Sgt. E C ROBERTS
AC1 G W ROBERTS
Mid.(FAA) G W ROBERTS
F/O R ROBERTS
Sgt. B L ROBERTSON
Sgt. F N ROBERTSON
F/Lt. A I ROBINSON
Sgt. D N ROBINSON
P/O G ROBINSON
F/O J C E ROBINSON
Sgt. J ROBINSON
S/Ldr. M ROBINSON
S/Ldr. M L ROBINSON
S/Ldr. M W S ROBINSON
F/O P B ROBINSON
Sgt. P E M ROBINSON
Sgt. P T ROBINSON
P/O F A ROBSHAW
F/Lt. N C H ROBSON
Sgt. H A C RODEN
F/O B J ROFE
F/O B A ROGERS
P/O E B ROGERS
Sgt. G W ROGERS
Sgt. W T E ROLLS
Sgt. A L ROMANIS
F/Lt. A H ROOK

F/O M ROOK
P/O G L ROSCOE
P/O E B M ROSE
F/O J ROSE
Sgt. J S ROSE
P/O S N ROSE
F/O A T ROSE-PRICE
S/Ldr. F E ROSIER
P/O A R ROSS
P/O J K ROSS
P/O J H ROTHWELL
Sgt. J H ROUND
Sgt. J ROURKE
Sgt. G W ROUSE
P/O J H ROWDEN
Sgt. P A ROWELL
F/Lt. R M B ROWLEY
F/O M E A ROYCE
F/Lt. W B ROYCE
Sgt. W S RUDDOCK
Sgt. C P RUDLAND
F/Lt. F W RUSHMER
Sgt. A G RUSSELL
Lt.(FAA) G F RUSSELL
P/O G H RUSSELL
F/Lt. H a'B RUSSELL
P/O J T RUSSELL
Sgt. C A RUST
F/Lt. P RUSTON
P/O R D RUTTER
Cpl. B RYALL
P/O D L RYALLS
F/Lt. E N RYDER
F/Sgt. H S SADLER
P/O N A SADLER
F/Lt. E F StAUBYN
Sgt. R G StJAMES-SMITH
F/O P C B StJOHN
F/O H N E SALMON

P/O W N C SALMOND
Sgt. E SALWAY
S/Ldr. J SAMPLE
Sgt. A SAMPSON
F/Lt. J G SANDERS
S/Ldr. P J SANDERS
Sgt. A K SANDIFER
Sgt. R E B SARGENT
Sgt. A R SARRE
S/Ldr. W A J SATCHELL
P/O C H SAUNDERS
S/Ldr. G A W SAUNDERS
Sgt. T W SAVAGE
Sgt. J E SAVILL
Sgt. C J SAWARD
S/Ldr. H C SAWYER
F/Sgt. J E SAYERS
P/O K SCHADTLER-LAW
P/O E C SCHOLLAR
P/O F H SCHUMER
F/Lt. L H SCHWIND
Sgt. A E SCOTT
P/O A M W SCOTT
S/Ldr. D R SCOTT
F/O D S SCOTT
Sgt. E SCOTT
Sgt. G W SCOTT
Sgt. J A SCOTT
F/Lt. R H SCOTT
F/O W J M SCOTT
F/O F D S SCOTT-MALDEN
F/O G E T SCRASE
Sgt. E W SEABOURNE
P/O L A SEARS
F/O D SECRETAN
F/O W J SEDDON
Sgt. R F SELLERS
F/O J B SELWAY
Sgt. B SENIOR

Sgt. J N SENIOR
Sgt. A SERVICE
Sgt. D A SEWELL
Sgt. M M SHANAHAN
P/O H R SHARMAN
Sgt. B R SHARP
P/O L M SHARP
Sgt. R J SHARP
Sgt. H SHARPLEY
Sgt. W G SHARRATT
P.O.(FAA) F J SHAW
F/O I G SHAW
P/O R H SHAW
Sgt. H F W SHEAD
Sgt. H SHEARD
Sgt. F W SHEPHERD
Sgt. F E R SHEPHERD
Sgt. J B SHEPHERD
P/O D C SHEPLEY
Sgt. W J P SHEPPARD
Sgt. E E SHEPPERD
Sgt. G E SHEPPERD
Sgt. S SHERIDAN
P/O T B A SHERRINGTON
P/O E A SHIPMAN
Sgt. S H J SHIRLEY
P/O N B SHORROCKS
F/O R U P SHUTTLEWORTH
Sgt. F A SIBLEY
Sgt. F H SILK
Sgt. W G SILVER
Sgt. G F SILVESTER
Sgt. R B SIM
P/O V C SIMMONDS
F/Lt. J W C SIMPSON
P/O L W SIMPSON
F/O P J SIMPSON
Sgt. I R SIMS
P/O J A SIMS

F/Lt. G L SINCLAIR
P/O J SINCLAIR
F/Lt. J E J SING
F/O W M SIZER
Sgt. V H SKILLEN
F/Lt. C D E SKINNER
F/Lt. S H SKINNER
Sgt. W M SKINNER
Sgt. J W SLADE
P/O D M SLATTER
Lt.(FAA) J W SLEIGH
Sgt. O K SLY
Sgt. J SMALLMAN
F/O T SMART
Sgt. A SMITH
Sgt. A D SMITH
P/O A J SMITH
S/Ldr. A T SMITH
F/Lt. C D S SMITH
P/O D N E SMITH
F/O D S SMITH
F/Lt. E B B SMITH
Sgt. E C SMITH
P/O E L SMITH
F/Lt. E S SMITH
Sgt. F SMITH
Sub/Lt.(FAA) F A SMITH
Sgt. G E SMITH
Sgt. H SMITH
Sgt. H SMITH
Sgt. K B SMITH
Sgt. L E SMITH
Sgt. L SMITH
Sgt. L H SMITH
P/O N H J SMITH
Sgt. P R SMITH
Sgt. P R SMITH
P/O R SMITH
Sgt. R C SMITH

F/Lt. R L SMITH
F/Lt. W A SMITH
Sgt. W B SMITH
F/Lt. W O L SMITH
P/O J L SMITHERS
Sgt. R SMITHSON
Sgt. R H SMYTH
P/O D M A SMYTHE
Sgt. G SMYTHE
F/O R F SMYTHE
W/O W G SNAPE
F/O V R SNELL
P/O W G SNOW
Sgt. E G SNOWDEN
Sgt. H J SOARS
Sgt. P A SOBEY
P/O J F SODEN
P/O N D SOLOMON
Sgt. L C SONES
Sgt. G SOUTHALL
Sgt. G A SOUTHORN
P/O J S SOUTHWELL
Sgt. A W P SPEARS
F/Lt. H SPEKE
S/Ldr. D G H SPENCER
Sgt. G H SPENCER
Sgt. A H SPIERS
Sgt. J H SPIRES
Sgt. M H SPRAGUE
Sgt. R A SPYER
Sgt. J W C SQUIER
P/O D A STANLEY
Sgt. L STAPLES
P/O M E STAPLES
Sgt. R C J STAPLES
S/Ldr. H M STARR
P/O C M STAVERT
Sgt. D J STEADMAN
Sgt. R M STEELE

F/Sgt. H STEERE
F/Sgt. J STEERE
P/O D STEIN
Sgt. J STENHOUSE
P/O H M STEPHEN
Sgt. C STEPHENS
F/Lt. M M STEPHENS
F/O I R STEPHENSON
P/O P J T STEPHENSON
F/O S P STEPHENSON
P/O E J STEVENS
Sgt. G STEVENS
F/O L W STEVENS
Sgt. R E STEVENS
Sgt. W R STEVENS
P/O P C F STEVENSON
Sgt. G A STEWARD
Sgt. C N D STEWART
F/O D G A STEWART
P/O D STEWART-CLARK
F/Lt. P A M STICKNEY
Sgt. R L STILLWELL
Sgt. E STOCK
Sgt. N J STOCKS
P.O.(FAA) W E J STOCKWELL
F/Lt. K M STODDART
P/O R W STOKES
Sgt. J STOKOE
Sgt. S STOKOE
F/Lt. C A C STONE
P/O D W A STONES
F/Lt. G E B STONEY
Sgt. D R STOODLEY
P/O J M STORIE
F/O J E STORRAR
P/O A J STORRIE
F/O W W STRAIGHT
Sgt. J M STRAWSON
S/Ldr. V C F STREATFEILD

Sgt. R R STRETCH	Lt.(FAA) E W T TAYLOUR	F/O J G TOPHAM	P/O A G WAINWRIGHT	F/O R McG WATERSTON	F/O N R WHEATCROFT
P/O C D STRICKLAND	Sgt. F J TEARLE	Sgt. D F TOUCH	F/O M T WAINWRIGHT	F/Lt. D H WATKINS	P/O N J WHEELER
F/Lt. J M STRICKLAND	P/O C B TEMLETT	P/O W TOWERS-PERKINS	Sgt. F W WAKE	P/O W C WATLING	Sgt. J WHELAN
Sgt. G A STROUD	Sgt. P H R R TERRY	S/Ldr. P W TOWNSEND	P/O H K WAKEFIELD	P/O A R WATSON	P/O M T WHINNEY
Sgt. M STUART	F/Sgt. P H TEW	Sgt. T W TOWNSHEND	P/O E C J WAKEHAM	P/O E J WATSON	Sgt. G A WHIPPS
P/O D R STUBBS	P/O D J THACKER	F/Lt. A J TRUMBLE	Sgt. S R E WAKELING	P/O E O WATSON	P/O H L WHITBREAD
Sgt. S G STUCKEY	Sgt. A J THEASBY	P/O A J J TRURAN	Sgt. G A WALKER	Sgt. J G WATSON	Sgt. A WHITBY
P/O J A P STUDD	F/Lt. J G THEILMANN	S/Ldr. R R S TUCK	F/O J H G WALKER	P/O L G WATSON	F/O B E G WHITE
P/O J E SULMAN	Sgt. A H THOM	F/O A B TUCKER	Sgt. N M WALKER	F/O R WATSON	S/Ldr. F L WHITE
Sgt. R G B SUMMERS	F/O C R D THOMAS	P/O B E TUCKER	F/O R J WALKER	Sgt. E L WATTS	Sgt. J WHITE
Sgt. F SUMNER	F/Lt. E H THOMAS	Sgt. F D TUCKER	Sgt. S WALKER	Sgt. R D H WATTS	Sgt. J WHITE
Sgt. C H S SUMPTER	F/Lt. F M THOMAS	Sgt. R Y TUCKER	P/O W L B WALKER	F/Lt. R F WATTS	Sgt. J S WHITE
Sgt. W A SUTCLIFFE	Sgt. G S THOMAS	F/O D R TURLEY-GEORGE	Sgt. F R WALKER-SMITH	F/Lt. B H WAY	P/O J W WHITE
F/O I W SUTHERLAND	P/O R C THOMAS	Sgt. R N TURNBULL	F/Lt. D S WALLEN	P/O L B R WAY	Sgt. R WHITE
F/O F B SUTTON	P/O R H THOMAS	F/Lt. D E TURNER	F/O R W WALLENS	F/Lt. P S WEAVER	F/Sgt. C WHITEHEAD
P/O F C SUTTON	Sgt. R T THOMAS	F/Sgt. G TURNER	Sgt. G A WALLER	F/Lt. P C WEBB	Sgt. R O WHITEHEAD
Sgt. H R SUTTON	P/O S R THOMAS	Sgt. R C TURNER	Sgt. P K WALLEY	P/O W F P WEBBER	Sgt. S A H WHITEHOUSE
P/O J R G SUTTON	P/O A R F THOMPSON	Sgt. L J TWEED	Sgt. D S WALLIS	Sgt. J WEBER	Sgt. J J WHITFIELD
P/O N SUTTON	P/O F N THOMPSON	Sgt. F J TWITCHETT	Sgt. H W WALMSLEY	Sgt. E R WEBSTER	P/O D WHITLEY
Sgt. G W SWANWICK	Sgt. J B THOMPSON	Sgt. E TYRER	Sgt. E WALSH	P/O F K WEBSTER	Sgt. A D WHITSON
Sgt. N T C SWANWICK	W/Cdr. J M THOMPSON	S/Ldr. F H TYSON	Sub/Lt.(FAA) R W M WALSH	Sgt. H G WEBSTER	Sgt. H G WHITTICK
F/O A T SWORD-DANIELS	Sgt. J R THOMPSON	Sgt. J W UNETT	Sgt. H WALTON	F/Lt. J T WEBSTER	F/O C D WHITTINGHAM
F/Sgt. C SYDNEY	P/O P D THOMPSON	F/Sgt. G C UNWIN	Sgt. W H WANT	F/Lt. J H WEDGWOOD	F/Lt. W H R WHITTY
Sgt. D B SYKES	Sgt. W W THOMPSON	S/Ldr. J D URIE	S/Ldr. E F WARD	Sgt. G V WEDLOCK	Sgt. P C WHITWELL
Sub/Lt.(FAA) J H C SYKES	F/Lt. J A THOMSON	Sgt. F USMAR	P/O J L WARD	F/O A N C WEIR	P/O P C WICKINGS-SMITH
P/O E J H SYLVESTER	P/O T R THOMSON	P/O G W VARLEY	Sgt. R A WARD	AC1 E WELCH	Sgt. A S WICKINS
Sgt. J E SYMONDS	F/Sgt. E R THORN	P/O J A C VENN	Sgt. W B WARD	P/O G H E WELFORD	F/O B J WICKS
Sgt. G W TABOR	Sgt. L A THOROGOOD	W/Cdr. J A VICK	Sgt. N P WARDEN	P/O M L WELLS	S/Ldr. S C WIDDOWS
P/O J MacG TALMAN	Sgt. P THORPE	P/O T A VIGORS	Sgt. P WARD-SMITH	F/O P H V WELLS	P/O J S WIGGLESWORTH
F/Sgt. J H TANNER	P/O A R TIDMAN	Sgt. L W VILES	Sgt. R T WARE	P/O G H A WELLUM	F/Lt. R D G WIGHT
Sgt. R F TATNELL	Sgt. J TILL	F/Lt. J W VILLA	P/O M P WAREHAM	P/O T D WELSH	Mid.(FAA) O M WIGHTMAN
P.O.(FAA) D E TAYLOR	Lt.(FAA) R C TILLARD	G/Capt. S F VINCENT	Sgt. P T WAREING	P/O D R WEST	Sgt. C WILCOCK
F/Lt. D M TAYLOR	F/O J TILLETT	Sgt. F F VINYARD	Sgt. W WARING	S/Ldr. H WEST	F/O E J WILCOX
Sgt. E F TAYLOR	P/O E G TITLEY	P/O A F VOKES	F/Lt. W H WARNER	Sgt. W H J WESTCOTT	P/O T S WILDBLOOD
Sgt. G N TAYLOR	P/O P A TOMLINSON	F/O J WADDINGHAM	F/O C WARREN	P/O G H WESTLAKE	P/O D C WILDE
Sgt. K TAYLOR	P/O R E TONGUE	P/O T S WADE	P/O D A P WARREN	P/O R D WESTLAKE	Sgt. G N WILKES
Sgt. N TAYLOR	Sgt. L V TOOGOOD	Sgt. J V WADHAM	AC1 J B W WARREN	F/O I B WESTMACOTT	Sgt. K A WILKINSON
P/O R TAYLOR	P/O F A TOOMBS	Sgt. P H WAGHORN	Sgt. S WARREN	Sgt. T E WESTMORELAND	F/Lt. R C WILKINSON
Sgt. R H W TAYLOR	Sgt. J R TOOMBS	Sgt. A D WAGNER	Sgt. T A WARREN	Sgt. B E P WHALL	S/Ldr. R L WILKINSON

Sgt. W A WILKINSON
F/O D A WILLANS
Sgt. P H WILLCOCKS
S/Ldr. C W WILLIAMS
F/O D C WILLIAMS
P/O D G WILLIAMS
F/Sgt. E E WILLIAMS
Sgt. G T WILLIAMS
P/O M A WILLIAMS
P/O T D WILLIAMS
P/O W D WILLIAMS
Sgt. R F WILLIS
Sgt. W C WILLS
Sgt. A A WILSDON
F/Lt. D S WILSON
P/O L D WILSON
Sgt. W WILSON
Sgt. W C WILSON
Sgt. V J WINGFIELD
F/Lt. C V WINN
P/O A L WINSKILL
Sgt. J WINSTANLEY
P/O D C WINTER
F/O R A WINTER
Sgt. J F WISE
P/O W D WISEMAN
P/O D H WISSLER
S/Ldr. E C WOLFE
Sgt. R WOLTON
Sgt. K R WOOD
Sgt. S V WOOD
Sgt. J E WOODGATE
P/O D N WOODGER
W/Cdr. A B WOODHALL
Sgt. N N WOODLAND
P/O C A WOODS-SCAWEN
F/O P P WOODS-SCAWEN
F/Lt. H J WOODWARD
F/O R S WOODWARD

Sgt. A W WOOLLEY
P/O E W WOOTTEN
F/O D K A WORDSWORTH
S/Ldr. J WORRALL
P/O P A WORRALL
Sub/Lt.(FAA) T V WORRALL
F/O K W WORSDELL
F/O A S WORTHINGTON
Sgt. H J WOTTON
Lt.(FAA) A J WRIGHT
F/O A R WRIGHT
Sgt. D L WRIGHT
Sgt. E W WRIGHT
Sgt. J WRIGHT
Sgt. K S WRIGHT
Sgt. R R WRIGHT
P/O W WRIGHT
LAC J P WYATT
F/O P WYATT-SMITH
P/O R E N E WYNN
P/O D S YAPP
Sgt. G YATES
Sgt. W YATES
Sgt. R L YORK
P/O C R YOUNG
P/O J H R YOUNG
F/Lt. J R C YOUNG
P/O M H YOUNG
Sgt. R C YOUNG

AUSTRALIA
F/O I N BAYLES
P/O C C BENNETT
F/Lt. R W BUNGEY
P/O F W CALE
F/O J R COCK
F/O A N CONSTANTINE
Sgt. V W J CROOK
P/O J D CROSSMAN

F/Lt. F W FLOOD
Sgt. D FOPP
F/O R L GLYDE
P/O A L HAMILTON
F/O H G HARDMAN
Sgt. K C HOLLAND
F/Lt. P C HUGHES
F/Lt. J C KENNEDY
S/Ldr. R B LEES
P/O B M McDONOUGH
P/O C A McGAW
F/O H C MAYERS
P/O W H MILLINGTON
Sgt. P J MOORE
F/O W S MOORE
F/Lt. C G C OLIVE
P/O J F PAIN
P/O V PARKER
F/Lt. R M POWER
F/Lt. C A PRITCHARD
F/Lt. R C REYNELL
F/Lt. D F B SHEEN
F/Lt. S C WALCH
F/Lt. L C WITHALL

BARBADOS
P/O A R deL INNISS

BELGIUM
P/O M S H C BUCHIN
Sgt. R E de CANNERT
d'HAMALE
P/O B M G de HEMPTINNE
P/O R G C de HEMRICOURT
de GRUNNE
P/O L J DEJACE
Sgt. R J G DEMOULIN
P/O F X E de SPIRLET
P/O G DIEU

P/O G L J DOUTREPONT
P/O H A C GONAY
Sgt. L. HEIMES
P/O L L G JAVAUX
P/O A R I G JOTTARD
P/O J C KIRKPATRICK
Sgt. O G LEJEUNE
P/O D A R G le ROY du
VIVIER
P/O R F F MALENGREAU
Sgt. A C A MICHIELS
P/O J H M OFFENBERG
P/O V ORTMANS
P/O J A L PHILIPPART
P/O L PREVOT
P/O C L ROMAN
P/O E G A SEGHERS
P/O A E A D J G Van Den
HOVE d'ERTSENRIJCK
P/O W Van LIERDE
P/O A A L Van
WAEYENBERGHE
Sgt. F A VENESOEN

CANADA
F/O C I R ARTHUR
Lt.(FAA) R S BAKER-FALKNER
F/Lt. R A BARTON
P/O P H BEAKE
F/O E W BEARDMORE
P/O R W G BELEY
P/O J BENZIE
F/Lt. H P BLATCHFORD
P/O C R BONSEIGNEUR
F/O J G BOYLE
F/O E C BRIESE
F/Lt. M H BROWN
P/O M K BROWN
P/O J BRYSON

P/O P BYNG-HALL
P/O A R McL CAMPBELL
P/O N N CAMPBELL
Sub/Lt.(FAA) J C
CARPENTER
F/O J C CARRIERE
P/O G C T CARTHEW
F/O E F J CHARLES
P/O J A J CHEVRIER
P/O G P CHRISTIE
P/O B E CHRISTMAS
P/O A C COCHRANE
P/O W C CONNELL
P/O G H CORBETT
F/Lt. V B CORBETT
P/O M C CORNER
F/O L E CRYDERMAN
P/O W A CUDDIE
F/Lt. R W DENISON
F/Lt. J-P J DESLOGES
P/O R H DIBNAH
F/O N D EDMOND
P/O H D EDWARDS
F/O R L EDWARDS
F/O A L EDY
P/O G J ELLIOTT
S/Ldr. A W FLETCHER
P/O E G FORD
P/O C G FRIZELL
P/O R C FUMERTON
F/Lt. L M GAUNCE
S/Ldr. J A G GORDON
F/O R D GRASSICK
F/Lt. H R HAMILTON
F/O B A HANBURY
F/Lt. T P HARNETT
F/O J S HART
P/O N HART
P/O D A HEWITT

F/O F W HILLOCK
F/O G G HYDE
P/O J T JOHNSTON
S/Ldr. J A KENT
F/O J W KERWIN
Sgt. J R KILNER
P/O J E P LARICHELIERE
P/O J B LATTA
F/O R G LEWIS
F/O T B LITTLE
F/O P W LOCHNAN
Sgt. R H LONSDALE
S/Ldr. J R MacLACHLAN
P/O J B McCOLL
F/Lt. G R McGREGOR
P/O W L McKNIGHT
S/Ldr. E A McNAB
F/O W B MacD MILLAR
P/O J A MILNE
P/O H T MITCHELL
F/O H deM MOLSON
F/O W H NELSON
F/O A D NESBITT
P/O H G NIVEN
F/O R W G NORRIS
F/Lt. P G St.G O'BRIAN
P/O A K OGILVIE
F/O J D PATTISON
P/O O J PETERSON
F/O P B PITCHER
Sgt. O W PORTER
P/O G R PUSHMAN
P/O H W REILLEY
F/Lt. E M REYNO
Sgt. L V P J RICKS
F/O B D RUSSEL
P/O K M SCLANDERS
F/O A W SMITH
F/Lt. F M SMITH

F/O J D SMITH
F/O R R SMITH
F/O R SMITHER
P/O H A SPRAGUE
F/O W P SPRENGER
P/O N K STANSFELD
F/Lt. H N TAMBLYN
F/O C W TREVENA
P/O A A G TRUEMAN
F/Lt. P S TURNER
P/O H C UPTON
P/O J R URWIN-MANN
F/O J A WALKER
F/O J R WALKER
P/O C A B WALLACE
P/O J J WALSH
P/O F S WATSON
P/O R R WILSON
F/Lt. J S YOUNG
F/O A McL YUILE
P/O A R ZATONSKI

CZECHOSLOVAKIA
S/Ldr. J AMBRUS
P/O J BARTOS
P/O V BERGMAN
Sgt. F A BERNARD
Sgt. V BREJCHA
P/O F BURDA
Sgt. F CHABERA
P/O E CIZEK
Sgt. V E CUKR
P/O F DOLEZAL
P/O J DUDA
Sgt. A DVORAK
Sgt. J DYGRYN
P/O F FAJTL
P/O E FECHTNER
P/O S FEJFAR

Sgt. V FOGLAR
P/O E A FOIT
Sgt. J FRANTISEK
Sgt. B FURST
P/O V GOTH
P/O J J HANUS
Sgt. O HANZLICEK
S/Ldr. A HESS
P/O J HIMR
Sgt. J HLAVAC
P/O A HLOBIL
Sgt. V HORSKY
P/O F HRADIL
Sgt. O HRUBY
Sgt. J HUBACEK
P/O J E HYBLER
P/O S JANOUCH
P/O J A JASKE
Sgt. V JICHA
F/Sgt. M JIROUDEK
F/Sgt. J KANIA
Sgt. J KAUCKY
Sgt. J KEPRT
Sgt. O KESTLER
F/Sgt. J KOMINEK
Sgt. M KOPECKY
Sgt. J KOPRIVA
Sgt. K KORBER
P/O F KORDULA
Sgt. J KOUKAL
Sgt. B KRATKORUKY
P/O M KREDBA
Sgt. J V KUCERA
Sgt. J KUCERA
Sgt. O KUCERA
Sgt. K M KUTTELWASCHER
P/O J MACHACEK
F/Lt. J M MALY
Sgt. M J MANSFELD

Sgt. F MAREK
P/O K MRAZEK
Sgt. O PAVLU
Sgt. J PIPA
Sgt. S PLZAK
Sgt. E M PRCHAL
Sgt. J PRIHODA
Sgt. R PTACEK
Sgt. R PUDA
Sgt. J RECHKA
P/O R B ROHACEK
F/Lt. F RYPL
Sgt. K SEDA
Sgt. J SIKA
Sgt. V SLOUF
Sgt. J STEFAN
Sgt. J STEHLIK
P/O J STERBACEK
F/Sgt. J STRIHAVKA
Sgt. J TRUHLAR
P/O A VASATKO
P/O A VELEBNOVSKY
P/O V VESELY
Sgt. F VINDIS
Sgt. J VOPALECKY
P/O A VRANA
P/O T VYBIRAL
P/O K J VYKOUKAL
P/O F WEBER
P/O V ZAORAL
Sgt. A ZAVORAL
Sgt. R ZIMA
P/O S ZIMPRICH

FRANCE
ADJ P M BLAIZE
ADJ H J BOUQUILLARD
ADJ Y J BRIERE
ADJ M P C CHORON

ADJ F H E J A
  DeLABOUCHERE
ADJ X deC DeMONTBRON
2/Lt. J-F DEMOZAY
Capt. C J M P deSCITIVAUX
  deGREISCHE
ADJ E F M L FAYOLLE
ADJ C P GUERIN
ADJ H G LAFONT
ADJ R G O J MOUCHOTTE
ADJ G C PERRIN

IRELAND
W/Cdr. F V BEAMISH
P/O B B CONSIDINE
F/Lt. R S J EDWARDS
F/O B E FINUCANE
P/O G J GROGAN
S/Ldr. H HARKNESS
F/O J A HEMINGWAY
F/Lt. N L IEVERS
F/Lt. J I KILMARTIN
P/O W W McCONNELL

JAMAICA
P/O H CAPSTICK

NEWFOUNDLAND
P/O R A HOWLEY

NEW ZEALAND
F/O J H L ALLEN
Sgt. M R ANDREWS
P/O G M BAIRD
F/O R E BARY
Sgt. J BAYLY
Sgt. A BENNISON
P/O J L BICKERDIKE
S/Ldr. M V BLAKE

Sgt. J S BRENNAN
F/O F N BRINSDEN
Sgt. R W BROOKMAN
P/O B W BROWN
Sgt. W R BURNS
Sgt. D L BURTON
P/O C R BUSH
Sgt. A CAMPBELL
Sgt. D B CAMPBELL
F/O B J G CARBURY
F/Lt. M K CARSWELL
Sgt. C CHRYSTALL
P/O E W G CHURCHES
S/Ldr. A E CLOUSTON
F/O W G CLOUSTON
P/O D G COBDEN
P/O B G COLLYNS
Sgt. J B COURTIS
P/O H H CRAWFORD
Sgt. E E CROKER
P/O J T DAVISON
Sgt. K DAWICK
F/Lt. A C DEERE
F/O V B de la PERELLE
Sgt. C R DURRANT
Sgt. H D P DYER
P/O E R EDMUNDS
P/O W T EIBY
Sgt. C S EMENY
Sgt. W G FENTON
F/Lt. T B FITZGERALD
F/O J FLEMING
Sgt. W T FLETCHER
Sgt. C L M FORSYTH
P/O A L FOWLER
P/O J R GARD'NER
F/O A A GAWITH
F/Lt. J A A GIBSON
Sgt. I A C GRANT

F/O C F GRAY
F/O J W HAMILL
F/O J C F HAYTER
P/O B H HERRICK
P/O M J HERRICK
P/O C H HIGHT
P/O H P HILL
Sgt. F G HINDRUP
P/O W H HODGSON
P/O P W HORTON
Sgt. D E HUGHES
P/O J S HUMPHREYS
Sgt. R J HYDE
S/Ldr. P G JAMESON
Sgt. G B JOHNSON
P/O J R KEMP
P/O R KIDSON
F/O M C KINDER
Sgt. R I LAING
P/O O E LAMB
P/O C E LANGDON
P/O K A LAWRENCE
S/Ldr. T G LOVELL GREGG
F/O H S LUSK
Sgt. R I McCHESNEY
Sgt. J A McDERMOTT
W/Cdr. H D McGREGOR
P/O E H McHARDY
P/O A G McINTYRE
P/O D C MACKENZIE
F/O J N MACKENZIE
F/O J C MARTIN
P/O W A MIDDLETON
Sgt. H R MITCHELL
F/Lt. N J MOWAT
Sgt. W J MURLAND
F/O H L NORTH
Sgt. T W OAKS
P/O E ORGIAS

Sgt. G C R PANNELL
Sgt. E E PARSONS
F/O J A PATERSON
P/O J G PATTISON
P/O J S PRIESTLEY
Sgt. J W PYE
Sgt. C C PYNE
F/O P W RABONE
Sgt. L A W RASMUSSEN
Sgt. C C REILLY
Sgt. L P RUSSELL
Sgt. W J SCOTT
P/O M M SHAND
P/O G M SIMPSON
P/O I S SMITH
P/O D J SPENCE
P/O R L SPURDLE
Sgt. N M STANGER
Sgt. D O STANLEY
P/O C STEWART
F/O J T STRANG
F/O K R SUTTON
F/O K W TAIT
Sgt. G S TAYLOR
F/Lt. R A THOMSON
P/O O V TRACEY
P/O R M TROUSDALE
P/O V B S VERITY
Sgt. J I B WALKER
F/Lt. D H WARD
P/O J WATTERS
P/O E P WELLS
F/O K V WENDEL
S/Ldr. E W WHITLEY
P/O D M WHITNEY
F/O R G WIGG
P/O W S WILLIAMS
Sgt. W O WILLIS
F/O D F WILSON

Sgt. R B M YOUNG
F/O R D YULE

POLAND
Sgt. T ANDRUSZKOW
F/Lt. W BARANSKI
Sgt. A BEDA
Sgt. M BELC
P/O B BERNAS
F/O J BOROWSKI
F/Lt. S BRZEZINA
Sgt. M BRZEZOWSKI
Sgt. J BUDZINSKI
F/O A CEBRZYNSKI
P/O S J CHALUPA
P/O M CHELMECKI
F/Lt. T CHLOPIK
P/O F CZAJKOWSKI
P/O J M CZERNIAK
F/Lt. J T CZERNY
P/O T CZERWINSKI
P/O S CZTERNASTEK
P/O J K M DASZEWSKI
Sgt. M B DOMAGALA
P/O B H DROBINSKI
F/O M DURYASZ
Sgt. S DUSZYNSKI
F/O J FALKOWSKI
P/O M FERIC
F/Lt. J FREY
F/O A K GABSZEWICZ
Sgt. P P GALLUS
P/O J GIL
Sgt. A GLOWACKI
P/O W J GLOWACKI
Sgt. F GMUR
P/O W GNYS
P/O M GORZULA
F/O B GROSZEWSKI

F/O F GRUSZKA
F/O B GRZESZCZAK
F/Lt. Z K HENNEBERG
P/O Z JANICKI
P/O J JANKIEWICZ
F/O W JANUSZEWICZ
F/Lt. F JASTRZEBSKI
Sgt. J JEKA
P/O E W JERECZEK
Sgt. S KARUBIN
P/O W E KARWOWSKI
P/O T W KAWALECKI
Sgt. S KITA
P/O S KLECZKOWSKI
Sgt. Z KLEIN
Sgt. W KLOZINSKI
Sgt. W KOSARZ
F/Lt. B K KOSINSKI
Sgt. J KOWALSKI
F/O J KOWALSKI
P/O F KOZLOWSKI
F/Lt. Z KRASNODEBSKI
P/O W KREPSKI
F/O W S KROL
P/O T L KUMIEGA
F/O Z KUSTRZYNSKI
F/Sgt. J KWIECINSKI
F/Lt. P LAGUNA
P/O S LAPKA
P/O W LAPKOWSKI
F/O W LAZORYK
P/O W LOKUCIEWSKI
F/O K LUKASZEWICZ
Sgt. A LYSEK
Sgt. M M MACIEJOWSKI
P/O J MACINSKI
Sgt. B MALINOWSKI
P/O J L MALINSKI
Sgt. M S MARCINKOWSKI

Sgt. A L MARKIEWICZ
P/O L MARTEL
P/O B MIERZWA
P/O W MIKSA
Sgt. K A MUCHOWSKI
Sgt. W MUDRY
S/Ldr. M MUMLER
P/O A R NARUCKI
P/O P NIEMIEC
P/O Z NOSOWICZ
P/O T NOWAK
Sgt. E J A NOWAKIEWICZ
F/O T NOWIERSKI
F/O Z OLENSKI
Sgt. B OLEWINSKI
S/Ldr. J ORZECHOWSKI
F/O P OSTASZEWSKI-
  OSTOJA
P/O A OSTOWICZ
Sgt. J PALAK
P/O J H PALUSINSKI
F/Lt. W PANKRATZ
F/O L W PASZKIEWICZ
Sgt. E PATEREK
P/O J P PFEIFFER
P/O S PIATKOWSKI
P/O E R PILCH
F/O M PISAREK
P/O K PNIAK
P/O J POPLAWSKI
P/O J RADOMSKI
P/O G RADWANSKI
Sgt. J A ROGOWSKI
P/O M ROZWADOWSKI
P/O W ROZYCKI
P/O W M C SAMOLINSKI
Sgt. W SASAK
F/O T SAWICZ
Sgt. A SEREDYN

Sgt. A SIUDAK
P/O H SKALSKI
P/O S SKALSKI
Sgt. H SKOWRON
P/O J J SOLAK
F/O M J STEBOROWSKI
P/O S STEGMAN
P/O F SURMA
Sgt. L SWITON
Sgt. W SZAFRANIEC
Sgt. E SZAPOSZNIKOW
P/O H SZCZESNY
Sgt. J SZLAGOWSKI
P/O W SZULKOWSKI
F/O J TOPOLNICKI
S/Ldr. W URBANOWICZ
P/O S WAPNIAREK
P/O A WCZELIK
Sgt. M WEDZIK
P/O S WITORZENC
P/O B A WLASNOWOLSKI
Sgt. A WOJCICKI
Sgt. M I WOJCIECHOWSKI
Sgt. S WOJTOWICZ
P/O Z T A WROBLEWSKI
F/Sgt. K WUNSCHE
P/O B WYDROWSKI
F/O W ZAK
Sgt. J ZALUSKI
P/O P ZENKER
P/O A ZUKOWSKI
P/O J E L ZUMBACH
P/O J ZURAKOWSKI

SOUTHERN RHODESIA
P/O J A G CHOMLEY
Sgt. C G HODSON
F/Lt. J B HOLDERNESS

SOUTH AFRICA
F/O N J M BARRY
F/Lt. W S BOWYER
F/O P R-F BURTON
S/Ldr. G F CHATER
P/O C A G CLARK
F/O I B DIFFORD
P/O G J DRAKE
F/O C W GOLDSMITH
P/O L W GRAHAM
P/O R H HAVILAND
F/O I B D E HAY
F/Lt. G D L HAYSOM
F/O M R HILL
F/O P H HUGO
S/Ldr. C B HULL
P/O A G LEWIS
S/Ldr. A G MALAN
F/O E J MORRIS
P/O J R S OELOFSE
F/O S R PEACOCK-
  EDWARDS
P/O F H POSENER
F/O B G STAPLETON
F/O B VanMENTZ
Sgt. T Y WALLACE
P/O A B WATKINSON

UNITED STATES
F/O D D BROWN
F/Lt. C R DAVIS
P/O A G DONAHUE
P/O W M L FISKE
P/O J K HAVILAND
P/O V C KEOUGH
P/O P H LECKRONE
P/O A MAMEDOFF
P/O E Q TOBIN

BATTLE OF BRITAIN HISTORICAL SOCIETY

The Society, a registered charity, was founded in 1996 to establish a forum for like-minded enthusiasts seeking to pursue their interest in the Battle of Britain. Air Commodore Peter Brothers, a Fighter Command pilot who flew in the battle, is President of the Society , and all surviving aircrew are offered honorary membership. Members receive a monthly newsletter, *Scramble*.

Three years ago, the Society launched a unique initiative to construct a Monument in central London, recording the names of the Allied airmen who fought in the battle in 1940. It was considered appropriate that the contribution of non-combat personnel. including groundcrew, WAAFs and members of the rescue services should be remembered too. London's Embankment provided the perfect setting for Paul Day's inspiring Monument and is a location easily reached by visitors to the capital.

We are also responsible for sponsoring prints and publications directly related to the story of the battle, in which our education programme plays an important part. To learn more of the objectives of the Society visit www.battleofbritain.net, or write to Battle of Britain Historical Society, P.O. Box 174, Royal Tunbridge Wells, Kent TN4 9FA, England.

ACKNOWLEDGEMENTS

The main task in compiling a historical account of the Battle of Britain has been to offer a balanced if essentially selective picture, which aspires to recapture the flavour of events as they occurred through vivid snapshots of personal recollection. It has been a task which, more than anything else, served to increase my admiration for the unique and decisive contribution of RAF Fighter Command.

This book would never have been published without the generous and considerable support given by Paul and Mary Raikes, Dame Simone Prendergast, Peter Blond, and Jane Graham Maw at the Graham Maw Literary Agency, whose judgement I have always respected so much.

I must single out Edward McManus, CEO of the Battle of Britain Historical Society for acceding to endless demands for rare and unpublished photographs; and to Winston G. Ramsey, editor of the authoritative *After the Battle* magazine, an important source for historians of the period, and Steven Torrington of the *Daily Mail* for providing many of them.

I am equally indebted to Lord Lichfield, Dilip Bannerjee of the Imperial War Museum, Shelley Fallows, Peter Vacher and – two of Churchill's 'Few' – Bunny Currant and Jack Riddle for the use of illustrations kindly given.

A particular note of thanks is due to Anne Wilson, whose unceasing benevolence during her impressive design of the book was invaluable; to intellectual property lawyers Rouse and Co. International; Jonathan Falconer for his significant comments on the manuscript, and Jeremy Snell at Butler and Tanner for his enthusiasm and support.

We were most fortunate in receiving permission to print extracts from the following: Dundas Papers (Lady Dundas); The Cecil Day Lewis Estate ('Battle of Britain' from *The Complete Poems of Day Lewis*, Stanford UP, 1995); Brian Kingcome (*A Willingness to Die*, Tempus Publishing 1999); Richard Hough and Denis Richards (*The Battle of Britain,* *The Jubilee History*, Hodder & Stoughton 1989); Ken MacKenzie (*Hurricane Combat*, CCB Aviation Books 2000); Geoffrey Page (*Shot Down in Flames*, Grub Street 1999); Matthew Parker (*The Battle of Britain, June-October 1940*, Headline 2001); Alfred Price (*The Hardest Day: Battle of Britain 1940*, Cassell Military 1988, and *Spitfire Story*, Weidenfeld & Nicholson 1992), both reprinted by kind permission of Orion Publishing; Peter Vacher (*Hurricane R4118*, Grub Street 2005); Geoffrey Wellum (*First Light*, Viking 2003).

Finally, I must thank Paul Day for providing photographs and commentary for the Monument he created. A fitting tribute to those we can truly believe were heroes.

RUPERT PRIOR, September 2005